- Do you experience negative feelings when your husband asks you to fix a meal?
- Do you get angry when your wife disagrees with you?
- Do you resent the fact that your husband is fulfilled sexually?
- Do you feel resentment when your wife is the center of attraction?

Whatever the questions . . . *The Measure of a Marriage* is designed to help you and your spouse not only to measure your marriage . . . but to improve it.

THE MEASURE OF A
MARRIAGE

GENE A. GETZ

Regal
Books

A Division of GL Publications
Ventura, CA U.S.A.

Other good reading by Gene A Getz:
The Measure of a Church
The Measure of a Man
The Measure of a Woman
The Measure of a Family

The translation of all Regal books is under the direction of GLINT. GLINT provides technical help for the adaptation, translation and publishing of books for millions of people worldwide. For information regarding translation contact: GLINT, P.O. Box 6688, Ventura, California 93006.

Scripture quotations, unless otherwise indicted, are from *The New American Standard Bible*, © The Lockman Foundation 1960, 1962, 1963, 1968, 1971, 1972, 1973, 1975. Used by permission. Other versions include:
NIV: New International Version, Holy Bible. Copyright © 1978 by New York International Bible Society. Used by permission.
KJV: Authorized King James Version.

Third Printing, 1983

Published by Regal Books Division, GL Publications
Ventura, California 93006
Printed in U.S.A.

Library of Congress Catalog Card No. 78-53356
ISBN 0-8307-0638-0

Contents

If you are studying this book as a couple or in a group, be sure to get a copy of *The Measure of a Marriage Workbook* from your local church supplier.

If You're Interested in Marriage, This Book Is for You

Most people *are* interested in understanding more about marriage—whether married or unmarried. And most people who *are* married are interested in improving their marriage.

Today most marriages are undergoing various degrees of stress for various reasons. First, all human relationships experience strain due to the realities of life. And marriage represents the most intimate human relationship of all, and is probably affected more than any other by the "realities of life." Consequently, *every* marriage undergoes degrees of stress.

However, there is yet another reason all marriages experience stress. Our present-day societal structures are groaning and creaking from various changes that are continually bombarding our cultural foundations. Since every marriage is an integral part of the total culture, these changes—philosophical, economic and technological—all affect society generally and marriages particularly. In fact, *all* changes in society precipitate crises. How we handle these crises depends to a great extent on our physiological resources, intellectual insights, psychological maturity and—last, but not least—our spiritual perspectives.

You may or may not classify yourself as religious. Most people do. But whatever your viewpoint, you probably already know that the Bible has some very significant things to say about marriage. In fact, our traditional views about marriage in our Western culture are pretty much rooted in Hebrew-Christian thought and practice as stated in both the Old and New Testaments. For most of us our beliefs, attitudes and actions are probably more influenced by biblical ideas than we realize.

But whatever your religious heritage, this entire study is designed to help you and your spouse not only to *measure* your marriage but to *improve* your marriage. Each segment begins with a biblical idea and then proceeds to give you extra-biblical insights, both psychologically and sociologically, to help you understand more fully yourself and your marriage partner. Practical projects help you make these truths and insights a part of your day-to-day experience as a husband and wife.

You *can* improve your relationship. No matter what degree of success or failure you are experiencing you can begin at that point and move forward. And if you are contemplating marriage this book will help you to enter that relationship with a more adequate perspective on the dynamics involved.

Gene A. Getz, Ph.D.

Introduction

How to Use This Book

First, you can read this book by yourself—as a married person or as a single. As a married person, even if your mate is not interested in reading it, you will gain insights that will help you to relate more effectively to your partner, consequently improving your relationship in some areas.

And remember! Improvement in *one* area tends to transfer and generalize to others. In fact, your mate may be so impressed with the changes in your life that he or she too may get involved in the study.

Second, you can study this book as a couple, working through the projects together. This is far more effective than merely reading it on your own. It will serve as a do-it-yourself marriage enrichment course.

Third, you can participate with a group of couples. In fact, the projects are designed to be used in three ways: (1) for *personal* study; (2) for *husband and wife* study; and (3) for a *couples' group* study.

AS A GROUP OF COUPLES

The projects in this book are designed to be both self-contained and/or sequential. For example, if you get involved in a group study, the Group Project is designed to be worked out *in the group* (see fig. 1, step 1). However, following each group session, you should also follow through as a husband and wife team by doing the Couple Project (step 2). And when working through the Couple Project, each of you will also need to work through the Personal Project (step 3). This of course is the ideal approach.

STEP 3 ◆ ━ ━ ━	STEP 2 ◆ ━ ━ ━	STEP 1
Personal	**Couple**	**Group**
Project	**Project**	**Project**

Figure 1—As a group of couples

AS A COUPLE

However, not every couple can be involved in a group. Therefore, as illustrated in figure 2, you can begin with the Couple Project (step 1), which will also involve you in the Personal Project (step 2). And of course an excellent project and goal for both of you—once you've worked through the projects designed for personal and couple use—is to share this experience with a group of couples (step 3).

STEP 2	STEP 1	STEP 3
Personal Project	Couple Project	Group Project

Figure 2—As a couple

AS AN INDIVIDUAL

It is possible however that your marital partner may not want to participate either in a group or with you in the couple projects. Therefore, you can benefit significantly by working through the personal projects (see fig. 3) which hopefully will help you to eventually encourage your mate to be involved in the projects with you (steps 2 and 3).

STEP 1 ➡	STEP 2 ➡	STEP 3
Personal Project	Couple Project	Group Project

Figure 3—As an individual

A Notebook

If you're involved in this study either as a *couple* or with a *group* of couples, you will want to purchase a copy of *The Measure of a Marriage Workbook* (also published by Regal Books). This notebook is designed to accompany this book. It includes special tear-out sheets consisting of evaluation scales for both husbands and wives, as well as guidelines for goal setting. In other words, it's very important that you secure this notebook. It is not supplementary, but an integral part of both the couple and group projects.

CHAPTER 1

Becoming One

If you conducted a little survey on your own and stopped people on the street in New York or Los Angeles, London or Paris and asked them where the idea of marriage came from, most would probably tell you that it supposedly began with Adam and Eve in the Garden of Eden. This would happen even more frequently in small towns and rural communities.

Whatever your personal interpretation of this fascinating Old Testament story, the Bible simply states that the Lord God created the original man and woman and brought them together to form a unique relationship which we call marriage. And many people in our culture go back to this story when discussing the origins of marriage.

Moses, that incomparable Jewish leader who led the children of Israel out of Egypt and into the Promised

Land, recorded the intriguing event when God created Eve from Adam's rib and summarized that event with these words: "For this cause a man shall leave his father and his mother, and shall cleave to his wife; *and they shall become one flesh*" (Gen. 2:24).[1]

Many years later another Jew named Jesus Christ was asked His views on marriage by the religious philosophers and professors of His day. He mentally reached back in antiquity and quoted Moses' very words: "For this cause a man shall leave his father and mother, and shall cleave to his wife; *and the two shall become one flesh*" (Matt. 19:5; see also Mark 10:7,8). And then for emphasis Jesus added—"Consequently they are *no more two, but one flesh*" (Matt. 19:6).

It should not surprise us that Paul the apostle (author of 13 New Testament books), when discussing the relationship that should exist between a husband and wife, also quoted Moses—*and* Jesus. Calling marriage a "great mystery" (which also refers to the relationship between Christ and Christians), Paul again stated God's plan word for word: "For this cause a man shall leave his father and mother, and shall cleave to his wife; *and the two shall become one flesh*" (Eph. 5:31).

F. Foulkes wrote that, "this statement from the creation story is the most profound and fundamental statement in the whole of Scripture concerning God's plan for marriage."[2] It is indeed a logical place to begin when studying the subject of marriage in order to gain, not only a contemporary viewpoint on husband/wife relationships, but an historic perspective as well.

One in Humanness

What did Moses, *and* Jesus, *and* Paul mean when they

stated that a man and woman "become one flesh"? First of all, remember that the apostle Paul identified it as a *mystery*. Most of us who are married can verify experientially the truth in Paul's statement. There are certain dimensions to this relationship between a man and a woman that are impossible to understand and explain. However, the Bible *and* personal experience give us enough data to draw some rather impressive conclusions.

How was "oneness" illustrated in the original creation?

When God first created Adam, there was no one with whom he could truly become "one flesh." There was no other *human being* with whom he could share his life. The implication is clear. It would take another person created in God's image—and Adam's image—to fill that unique role. This is what God meant when He said that He would make a "helper *suitable*" (Gen. 2:18). This literally means "a help of his like," that is, "a helping being, which, as soon as he sees it, he may recognize himself."3

This was why Adam exclaimed when he first saw Eve: "This is now bone of my bones, and flesh of my flesh; she shall be called Woman, because she was taken out of Man" (Gen. 2:23).

Adam recognized that Eve was like him. Though she was uniquely female, she looked like him, talked like him, walked like him and smiled like him. She was his complement. He could relate to her as to no other living creature. She was another *human being*.

God had uniquely set the stage for this experience. Before creating Eve from Adam's rib, the Lord had arranged for him to name all of the animals that were already created. And as Adam named each creature, he did so with keen understanding of the nature of each one. In the process he discovered that there was no creature like himself (see Gen. 2:20). Consequently, when his eyes first fell on Eve—undoubtedly a beautiful and un-blemished creation—there was no doubt in his mind as to their affinity. In common parlance, the "chemistry" was right, which was far more than sexual. She was a unique creation, physically, psychologically and spiritually, just as he was.

One in Sexuality

But there's more! Eve was indeed *one* with Adam because she was literally taken from his side. Part of his very physical body became part of Eve's physical body. And before they were ever joined together sexually, they were already, in God's eyes, "one flesh."

How was "oneness" illustrated after the original creation?

After God created Adam and Eve, what caused a man and woman to become "one flesh" in God's eyes? First, understand that there is a unique relationship between *all* men and women who are ever born into this world. Ever since God created the first man and woman, every male and female reflect the same unity. *Together,* we are made in God's image (see Gen. 1:27). And together we reflect His image and His creative handiwork.

But there is an even more unique relationship that God intended. Though He certainly planned for all human beings (male and female) to fellowship with one another and to relate to one another because of the ongoing "one-ness" inherent in the original creation, there is yet another "oneness" referred to in the Bible—the oneness that exists between a husband and a wife. And that oneness is reflected in God's eyes when a man joins himself to a woman through the act of sexual intercourse. In this God-created consummation we see the original creation story illustrated again and again throughout history. In God's eyes a man and woman become ''one flesh.''

That God views sexual intercourse as a means by which a man becomes one with a woman (and vice versa) is emphasized by Paul in his letter to the Corinthians. These people were converted to Christianity out of a pagan culture where prostitution was a very real part of their religious life. Some of these new Christians initially continued in their old ways, visiting the pagan temples (and no doubt other places) where these women were readily available. Paul exhorted them in no uncertain terms against such a practice. ''Do you not know that your bodies are members of Christ?'' he asked. ''Shall I then take away the members of Christ and make them members of a harlot? *May it never be!* Or do you not know that the one who *joins* himself to a harlot is *one body* with her?'' (1 Cor. 6:15,16).

At this point Paul once again quotes Moses, *''The two will become one flesh''* (1 Cor. 6:16).

Taken in context there's no way to misinterpret Paul's statement. It is possible in God's eyes to become ''one flesh'' with more than one man or woman through the act of sexual intercourse, and this, the Bible teaches, is not God's will.

Isn't ''oneness'' more than physical unity?

The answer to this question is a definite yes. But in God's eyes, a unique unity takes place when a man and woman join in sexual union, whether it be a permanent or a promiscuous relationship. God's perfect will is that it be a *permanent* marriage, involving one man and one woman, reflecting the original creation. That is why Jesus also said to the religious philosophers of His day—"What therefore God has joined together, let not man separate" (Matt. 19:6).

One in Spirituality

What else is involved in this "oneness"?

Another facet of oneness can best be illustrated with the way the Bible describes Christian conversion. A person becomes a Christian by placing his faith in Jesus Christ for *personal* salvation. At that moment he becomes *one with Christ*. In this sense, each of us individually and all Christians collectively are "married" to Christ. Obviously, this is figurative language, but it is the very picture Paul painted in his Ephesian letter when discussing the interweaving relationship that exists between a husband and wife (see Eph. 5:22,23,32) as well as between Christ and His followers.

However, becoming "one with Christ" at conversion—when we personally receive Christ as Saviour (see John 1:12)—does not mean that our unity with Christ is *experientially* complete. It is true that God views us as *one* with Christ the moment we become a true believer. But to experience that unity in all of its fullness is yet another matter. As long as Christians are on earth we have the potential to grow in our relationship with Jesus Christ, personally and corporately, and the Bible teaches that someday we will be ultimately one with Him in heaven. The process will be complete. In the book of Revelation this ultimate experience is called the "marriage supper."

To a certain extent this process should also be true in a literal marriage, although this human relationship, according to Jesus, will terminate once we leave this earth.

We will no longer need this kind of human relationship to be fulfilled and happy. Jesus Christ will be all that we need. But while on earth our spiritual relationship with Christ illustrates our relationship with our marital partner. The act of intercourse, in God's eyes, indeed makes a man and woman "one flesh." But it is designed to be only a beginning point in a great adventure in getting to know each other not only physically but psychologically and spiritually. True *experiential* unity and oneness are yet future for a newly married couple. Like our *total* relationship with Christ, our *total* relationship with our husband or wife must be carefully nurtured and developed. Only then will we begin to *experience* true oneness.

Notes

1. Italics added. Hereafter all italics in Scripture quotations are added by the author for emphasis.
2. F. Foulkes, *The Epistle of Paul to the Ephesians* (Grand Rapids: Wm. B. Eerdmans Publishing Company, 1963), p. 161.
3. C.F. Keil and F. Delitzsch, *The Pentateuch* (Grand Rapids: Wm. B. Eerdmans Publishing Company, n.d.), p. 86.

CHAPTER 2

An Exercise in Becoming One

In our culture today more has been written about sexual unity than any other aspect of marriage. For some marriage partners, attaining mutual satisfaction physically has become a constant obsession. And usually this is attempted by experimenting with all kinds of physiological techniques found in a proliferation of sex manuals.

Don't misunderstand! Anyone who has counseled husbands and wives who are having sexual problems cannot ignore the value of learning various sexual techniques. Even in an enlightened society, there is still a great deal of ignorance regarding sexual physiology and technique. And later in this book we'll discuss some of these intimate aspects of marital life and how together you might improve your sex life.

Unfortunately, this kind of advice in itself is not the

key to unity and truly becoming one in a marriage relationship. In God's sight, when a man and woman are joined in a sexual union they *are* one, whether or not it is personally or mutually satisfying. But marital unity that is *total*—physical, psychological and spiritual—involves a process that takes time, insight, sensitivity and effort. And it is in this larger context that sexual unity which *is* mutually satisfying also takes place. Without this broader setting, even sexual satisfaction can become meaningless and eventually unsatisfactory. All the sex techniques in the world, without total unity, leave a marriage in shambles.

Because this is true the major part of this study is designed to help you, as a couple, develop total unity in marriage. So, let's get started!

Note: These projects are divided into three sections: (1) for individuals; (2) for couples; and (3) for groups of couples. However, each section builds on the other. In other words, if you are reading and working through this book as a *couple,* be sure to read carefully the section written for *individuals.* If you are in a *group* be sure to read the sections for *individuals* and *couples.*

AS AN INDIVIDUAL

If you are reading this book on your own (and you should be, even if you are working through it as a couple or in a group), read the following suggestions carefully.

Let's begin with a question. *How well do you really know your present or future marital partner?*

To discover the answer to this question, structure an opportunity to ask your mate (or future mate) some questions. Prepare yourself psychologically to really *listen* to what your partner says—that is, don't be defensive or emotionally resistant. Just listen, whether or not you "emotionally" agree with what is said.

Warning! This suggestion is particularly relevant for men who often tend to be more threatened and defensive than women when it comes to discussing marital problems.

Let me illustrate this point. On one occasion I was speaking at a pastor's breakfast sponsored by a Christian bookstore. The owner's wife (who also helped manage the bookstore) came to me and pointed out a paragraph I had written in an earlier book entitled *The Measure of a Woman*, which reads as follows:

"Most men find it difficult to listen to their wives share feelings of unhappiness and resentment. It is very threatening. But the fact is, it is only as the husband learns to know what his wife's needs are that he can meet those needs. There *must* be communication."[1]

"Gene," she said, "I encounter this problem more than any other in talking with women. Many husbands just will not listen to their wives when they try to share their negative feelings."

Unfortunately, she is right. But it's not just a man's problem. Some wives won't listen to their husbands either. Perhaps a woman's greatest weakness is not that she won't lend an ear, but she "listens" without *feeling* any real concern.

For example, Jane tells Bill she wants to hear about his work—his problems, his concerns, his frustrations. Her problem, however, is that she yawns while he's talking and when he's through she says, "That's too bad. Thanks for telling me," and then goes about her business or falls asleep.

Obviously, she hasn't *really* listened to Bill. And he

knows it. The problem is not defensiveness, as Bill's might be, but rather she's really not very interested. She's simply trying to use a technique that has not become a part of her internal concern and love for Bill.

If you're really going to listen to your husband or wife, you must *really* listen—nondefensively, intently, objectively and with feeling. You must not even allow yourself to think about how you are going to answer or respond. You will have plenty of time *after* you have listened to decide what you're going to say. In fact, if you are really listening, you'll be able to formulate your response more adequately *after* you have listened.

If you are not studying this book with your mate or in a group of couples, plan a time and find a place that is most conducive for asking your mate the questions that follow. Keep in mind that both of you should not be physically tired or psychologically on edge. In fact, the best time is when things generally are the most relaxed and comfortable in your marriage.

Warning: Don't be sneaky about this project. Be open and honest. You might say, "I've been reading this book entitled, *The Measure of a Marriage,* and there are several questions the author suggests that I ask my mate so as to learn more about myself and my relationship with you. I've been looking for an opportunity to ask you these questions. Do you mind if I ask them now or would there be a better time?"

These questions are arranged in a very important order. They move progressively from what are generally nonthreatening questions to more threatening ones. It's important that you follow this order. It will help the one *asking* the questions and the one *answering* the questions to be more sensitive, honest and nondefensive. (For couples, see *The Measure of a Marriage Workbook*.)

1. If you could point out *one thing* about me that pleases you the most, what would it be?

2. What would you say is my greatest strength?

3. How can I help you be a more fulfilled person?

4. What one thing in my personality or behavior pattern causes you the most emotional difficulty?

5. If you could change one thing about me, what would it be?

AS A COUPLE

If you are studying this book together as a husband and wife (or an engaged couple) you are already ahead of the game. Decide on a time and place to be alone for at least an hour.

Step 1—Take 10 minutes to silently record your answers to the following questions (Exercise 1 in *The Measure of a Marriage Workbook*).[2]

1. If you could point out one thing about your mate that pleases you the most what would it be? Why?

2. What would you say is your mate's greatest strength? Explain why.

3. How can your mate help you be a more fulfilled person?

4. What one thing in your mate's personality or behavior pattern causes you the most difficulty? Explain why.

5. If you could change one thing about your mate, what would it be?

Step 2—Share your answers with each other, using the following sequence:

Husband: Share the answers to question 1 with your mate.
Wife: Share the answers to question 1 with your mate.

Husband: Share the answer to question 2 with your mate.
Wife: Share the answer to question 2 with your mate.

Husband: Share the answer to question 3 with your mate.
Wife: Share the answer to question 3 with your mate.

Husband: Share the answers to question 4 with your mate.
Wife: Share the answers to question 4 with your mate.

Husband: Share the answer to question 5 with your mate.
Wife: Share the answer to question 5 with your mate.

NOTE: It is important that you not discuss the answers to these questions the first time through. Just listen to each other share answers. Both of you need time to reflect and develop objectivity. It is very important that you do not respond even though you want to—especially in a negative sense. Attempt to even avoid nonverbal reactions, such as looking away in disgust, or just looking away.

Alternate Suggestion: If you have extreme difficulty communicating in your marriage, you may need to simply let your mate read your answers to the questions and then wait a couple days to discuss them.

Additional Suggestion: If what your mate is saying is too painful to handle, simply extend your open hand in a "please stop" position indicating you cannot bear to hear more at this moment. With this nonverbal gesture you are simply asking for time to build up your emotional tolerance. You may need to wait until another time to regain your composure. As marital partners, respect and honor this request without indicating you feel it is a weakness. However, if you use this method try to never use it as a cop-out or escape from facing reality. If you do, you will never solve your marital problems.

Step 3—Now that you have shared your thoughts with each other without verbal reactions, go back and respond to each other's answers. Ask your partner for more clarification and elaboration. Be positive. Try to hear as much as you can so as to know how your mate really thinks and feels. If one or the other of you is not thinking clearly, there will be plenty of opportunity to state your own opinions in the projects to follow.

AS A GROUP OF COUPLES: Leader's Instructions

1. Separate into small groups of four or five in each group. Men and women should be in separate groups.

2. Have each group appoint a leader and a recorder.

3. Spend 10 minutes having each group of men answer the five questions for husbands and each group of women answer questions for wives.

4. Spend 20 to 30 minutes having each group recorder report the answers to the total group.

5. Agree that there will be no discussion or interaction during this first session—just reporting.

Note—There will inevitably be off-the-cuff comments that will be humorous. This is normal and helps break any tension that may exist. However, there should be no serious discussion or rebuttal during this first session.

Instruct those in the small groups to answer the following questions non-personally after going over the biblical material in chapter 1 and the first part of chapter 2. Rephrase the questions as follows:

Questions for Wives

1. If you could point out *one* thing about the *average* husband that pleases the *average* wife the most, what would it be? Why?

2. What is the greatest strength of the *average*

husband in today's culture? Why is this considered a strength?

3. How could the *average* husband help the *average* wife be a more fulfilled person? Explain.

4. What one personality factor in the *average* husband causes the most emotional difficulty in the *average* marriage? Explain why.

5. If you could change one thing about the *average* husband, what would it be?

Questions for Husbands

1. If you could point out *one* thing about the *average* wife that pleases the *average* husband the most, what would it be? Why?

2. What is the greatest strength of the *average* wife in today's culture? Why is this considered a strength?

3. How could the *average* wife help the *average* husband be a more fulfilled person? Explain.

4. What one personality factor in the *average* wife causes the most emotional difficulty in the *average* marriage? Explain why.

5. If you could change one thing about the *average* wife, what would it be?

Couple Assignment

Following the group process, assign couples to go home and *personalize* this group project in their own marriage by completing the three-step project on pages 26-28 under the title, AS A COUPLE, completing the worksheets in their own copy of *The Measure of a Marriage Workbook*.

Step 1—*Plan a Time*

As a couple spend a moment discussing with each

other a time when you can get together this coming week to work through the steps in the project for wives and for husbands for chapter 2. Find a place where you can get away from the house and the children. For example, have breakfast out and then work through the steps; or find a quiet place where you will be uninterrupted for a couple of hours.

Step 2—*Sign a Contract*

Following is a simple contract. As a couple, sign it, agreeing to commit yourselves to work through the projects together in this book. Though it may appear like a first-grade assignment, remember that some of us are still in the "first grade" in our marriages. But even as you consider yourself "in college" in your marital process, a contractual commitment of this nature is very helpful in following through when the pressures of other things tend to sidetrack us from our prior commitments.

With God's help we covenant together to attend this class on marriage and/or to work through the projects in this book.

Signed _____
　　　　　　　　　Husband

Signed _____
　　　　　　　　　Wife

Date _____

Notes

1. Gene A. Getz. *The Measure of a Woman* (Ventura, CA: Regal Books, 1977), p. 79.
2. *The Measure of a Marriage Workbook* (Ventura, CA: Regal Books, 1980) is available from your local church supplier.

CHAPTER 3

Leaving Father and Mother

Moses' original statement about marriage, which was reiterated by Jesus and Paul, contains another very significant principle for measuring a marital relationship. Not only do a man and woman become "one flesh" with unbounding potential for experiential unity and oneness, but the Bible also says: "For this cause a man [and woman] *shall leave his father and mother*" (Eph. 5:31).

In the most literal sense the Bible is simply referring to leaving certain established relationships with one family and starting another. It is only logical that a man and woman cannot become truly "one" in a practical sense unless they break certain ties with their parents and establish their own enduring relationship.

But this statement has profound implications beyond

just literal separation. In fact, it may be true that the real meaning is more related to "emotional" than "physical" separation. The facts are that children in biblical settings who separated from their parents did not necessarily move away from their parents. In their culture, they often lived under the same roof or right next door. The extended family was a part of their societal structures.

I remember visiting the Pompeii exhibit when it was on display in Dallas, Texas. As you'll remember, this Roman city was once a thriving metropolis before it was buried in A.D. 70 under tons of volcanic ash from erupting Mount Vesuvius. As you study the architectural designs of homes in that city—many of which have been carefully and painstakingly excavated by archaeologists—you can see how these structures reflect the concept of the extended family. One home particularly was featured, obviously owned by a very well-to-do family in Pompeii. The home included numerous rooms and sections where family members eventually set up their own housekeeping when they were married. In a sense *all* the members of the family lived under one roof, but there were also many homes within a home.

Although the trend in our twentieth-century culture is more toward geographical separation of parents and their married children, there are times, for economic or other reasons, when people do live together as multiple families. Close geographic proximity can make it more difficult to "leave father and mother" in the true and most profound sense of what that means.

Developing Unhealthy Dependence

For example, Bill and Mary are newly-married. Because Mary's parents have a large home, and because the newlyweds are trying to finish college, Mary's parents have invited them to live with them.

Is this wrong? Not necessarily. However, there's a problem. Bill, like most young men who marry early, has certain vulnerabilities. He knows Mary's parents are relatively well-to-do and are very unselfish with their material possessions. Consequently, under the financial pressures and the demands of college, Bill is becoming more and more dependent on his wife's parents to meet their material needs. Since he has not had to face the realities of life and his own responsibilities to support and care for Mary, he is not growing and maturing in this aspect of his life.

Will this turn out bad? Again, not necessarily. It all depends. But it has certain potential dangers that could eventually blow the lid off this new marriage.

For example, because of Bill's attitudes and behavior, Mary could be developing resentful feelings toward her husband which could eventually erupt. Or she could continue to harbor these feelings, never expressing them, and go into a state of depression.

Bill could also develop some very bad habit patterns both emotionally and volitionally. Life is filled with threatening responsibilities and having to face them later in life doesn't make it easier. But the temptation is always there to rely on good old Dad and Mom to help them out in financial binds.

Then, too, living with parents who are well-to-do makes it emotionally difficult for newly-married couples to eventually live in a small, sparsely-furnished apartment that is commensurate with their income. For most young couples starting out it will take a number of years—as it did their parents—to have sufficient resources to live more comfortably.

On the other hand, this does not mean that parents who are able should not be considerate of their married children and help them meet their needs. But should their help become a stumbling block in their children's marital adjustments, they must face this problem head-on. The most loving thing parents can do is to adjust *their* behavior so as to help both children "leave father and mother" and to establish their own home, responsibly and successfully. Furthermore, a young couple who sees a dependency syndrome developing should initiate the break themselves if their parents do not, regardless of how extremely painful at the time. Ultimate happiness is far more important than immediate comfort.

Immature Parents

There's another side to this problem. Sometimes close proximity brings out the immaturity in parents rather than in their children. For example, Tom and Jane are living next door to his parents. Tom is an only son and, though his mother loves Jane, down deep she has never felt there would ever be a girl quite good enough for her son (a rather common emotion for most mothers). Try as she might to overcome these feelings, she struggles with them every day. Unfortunately, close proximity visualizes Jane's inadequacies as a young bride and homemaker, and this only accentuates her mother-in-law's emotional problem.

Unfortunately, Tom's mother can't cover up her feelings. Jane is threatened by it all. Furthermore, Tom, as a young husband who also loves his mother, is slowly becoming convinced through her subtle innuendos that maybe Jane was a poor choice after all. For one thing, he can't quite seem to understand why his young working wife can't keep up the home as well as his older nonworking mother.

Obviously, this marriage is headed for serious problems because of close proximity. But again, all of us can point to children who *do* live next door or in the same house with their parents for a while with very few, if any, problems. But the principle of "leaving father and mother" is a valid one and both parents and children should face the issue immediately and make whatever changes are necessary. Generally, it is advisable in our culture to establish a certain degree of physical and geographical separation in order to avoid any potential problems. Because of the very nature of life, most of us, both parents and children, have a sufficient number of hang-ups to make us vulnerable. At this point an old adage is very appropriate: "An ounce of prevention is worth a pound of cure."

Emotions and Transference

When speaking of hang-ups it's important to realize that most of us have "emotional spillovers" from our home life that transfer to our mates and make it difficult to truly "leave father and mother." In fact, the phenomenon is inevitable regardless of how ideal our childhood experiences. All mothers and wives and fathers and husbands have many things in common.

Let me illustrate. Before he married, John's *mother* washed his clothes, made his bed, cooked his meals, and kept up the house. Now he's married and his wife, Sally, washes his clothes, makes his bed, cooks his meals and keeps up the house. Though Sally is involved in performing the same functions as John's mother used to, she does things differently. For one thing, she's not quite as efficient. She doesn't organize his socks the way his mother did, and sometimes she doesn't have the bed made up when he gets home from work. And her meal schedule is not as regular. These similar functions combined with the dissimilar procedures irritate John no end. He finds himself emotionally reacting to Sally and constantly compares her openly to his mother. This, of course, makes Sally furious. In fact, it makes her want to do the opposite.

Sally's problems are also aggravated by the fact that her husband, John, also reminds her of *her father*, who was always picking on *her* mother, putting her on a performance standard and reminding her that she did not measure up to *his* own mother.

This process is often at least partially subconscious. There are times when things irritate us about our mates that we don't really understand. Subconsciously over the years we have repressed certain feelings and emotions which we had toward our parents. Unknown to us we subtly transfer these covert emotions to a husband or wife. This can happen even though we have been reared in a relatively happy home situation.

I remember this process at work in my own life. After I was married I experienced certain spontaneous negative feelings toward my wife when she would ask me to do certain things—particularly if she expressed her desires with a certain tone of voice. It wasn't until years later while visiting my parents' home that I began to see the connection. I found myself—during that visit—reacting to my mother emotionally just as I had been reacting to my wife. I had come "full circle." Old emotional memories suddenly came to the surface. I clearly saw the source of my more recent emotional feelings and reactions toward my wife. They had been there all along at a subconscious level. In reality, when I reacted to my wife's requests I was reacting to my mother. Those reactions did not necessarily relate to whether or not I loved or respected my mother, which I did and still do. They were *natural* feelings I had not understood or dealt with properly as I was growing up.

CHAPTER 4

An Exercise in Leaving Parents

How well do you understand the emotional dynamics involved in your own marriage? To what extent have you actually "left" your father and mother psychologically? Understanding the answers to these questions is the place to start in isolating problems and then solving them. Personal insight is absolutely essential, and this chapter is designed to help you gain that insight.

AS AN INDIVIDUAL

The following evaluation scales will help you isolate areas that need attention. The statements focus on three areas: Dependence vs. Independence, Parental Maturity, Emotional Transference for the Wife and Emotional Transference for the Husband. Circle the number that best describes your personal situation.

Dependence vs. Independence

	Never	Seldom	Sometimes	Frequently
1. When I feel *in-security* I have a strong desire to share it with my mother.	1	2	3	4
2. When I get *angry* at my mate I have a strong desire to tell my mother.	1	2	3	4
3. When I get *lonesome* I have a strong desire to visit my mother.	1	2	3	4
4. When my mate *misunderstands* me I have a strong desire to talk with my mother.	1	2	3	4
5. When I have problems with my *children* I have a strong desire to seek my mother's advice.	1	2	3	4

	Never	Seldom	Sometimes	Frequently
6. When we run out of *money* I have a strong desire to ask my mother for financial help.	1	2	3	4
7. When I feel *insecurity* I have a strong desire to share it with my father.	1	2	3	4
8. When I get *angry* at my husband/wife, I have a strong desire to tell my father.	1	2	3	4
9. When I get *lonesome* I have a strong desire to visit with my father.	1	2	3	4
10. When my husband/wife *misunderstands* me I have a strong desire to talk with my father.	1	2	3	4

	Never	Seldom	Sometimes	Frequently
11. When I have problems with my *children* I have a strong desire to seek my father's advice.	1	2	3	4
12. When we run short of *money* I have a strong desire to ask my father for financial help.	1	2	3	4

Parental Maturity

	Never	Seldom	Sometimes	Frequently
1. My mother communicates with me to see how I'm doing in our marriage.	1	2	3	4
2. My mother criticizes my mate.	1	2	3	4
3. My mother sends me money.	1	2	3	4
4. My mother criticizes me.	1	2	3	4

	Never	Seldom	Sometimes	Frequently
5. My mother is upset if I don't contact her regularly.	1	2	3	4
6. My mother is quite disturbed if we visit my mate's parents more often than we visit them.	1	2	3	4
7. My father communicates with me to see how I'm doing in my marriage.	1	2	3	4
8. My father criticizes my mate.	1	2	3	4
9. My father sends me money.	1	2	3	4
10. My father criticizes me.	1	2	3	4
11. My father is upset if I don't contact him regularly.	1	2	3	4

	Never	Seldom	Sometimes	Frequently
12. My father is quite disturbed if we visit my mate's parents more often than we visit them.	1	2	3	4

Emotional Transference
For the Wife:

	Never	Seldom	Sometimes	Frequently
1. When my husband asks me to wash his clothes I feel negative.	1	2	3	4
2. When my husband asks me to sew a button on his clothes I feel negative.	1	2	3	4
3. When my husband asks me to fix a meal I feel negative.	1	2	3	4
4. When my husband asks me to make love I feel negative.	1	2	3	4

	Never	Seldom	Sometimes	Frequently
5. When my husband asks me to overcome a habit I experience negative feelings.	1	2	3	4
6. When my husband asks me to help him with his work I feel negative.	1	2	3	4
7. When my husband asks me to run an errand I experience negative feelings.	1	2	3	4
8. When my husband asks me to keep a certain time schedule I experience negative feelings.	1	2	3	4
9. When my husband disagrees with me I get angry.	1	2	3	4

	Never	Seldom	Sometimes	Frequently
10. When my husband makes a suggestion to me I get emotionally upset.	1	2	3	4

For the Husband:

	Never	Seldom	Sometimes	Frequently
1. When my wife asks me to help with the dishes I experience negative feelings.	1	2	3	4
2. When my wife asks me to carry out the garbage I experience negative feelings.	1	2	3	4
3. When my wife asks me to help with the housework I experience negative feelings.	1	2	3	4
4. When my wife asks me to show affection toward her I experience negative feelings.	1	2	3	4

	Never	Seldom	Sometimes	Frequently
5. When my wife asks me to overcome a habit I feel negative.	1	2	3	4
6. When my wife asks me to watch the children I feel negative.	1	2	3	4
7. When my wife asks me to account for the money I spend I feel negative.	1	2	3	4
8. When my wife asks me to maintain a certain time schedule I feel negative.	1	2	3	4
9. When my wife disagrees with me I get angry.	1	2	3	4
10. When my wife makes a suggestion to me I get emotionally upset.	1	2	3	4

As an individual, study your answers on these three scales. What can *you* do to improve your marriage, even though your mate is not particularly interested?

Suggestion: Share the results of your self-evaluation with a mature friend or competent Christian counselor. Seek their advice. Have them help you evaluate your objectivity regarding your marriage.

AS A COUPLE

Step 1—Make sure both of you have completed the three evaluation quizzes, Exercises 2, 3 and 4 in *The Measure of a Marriage Workbook*.

Step 2—Use the following questions to evaluate your responses. Each of you should take at least 10-15 minutes to write your observations in Exercise 5 in *The Measure of a Marriage Workbook*.

Dependence vs. Independence

1. As a wife are there any areas where you are overly *dependent* on your mother? Your father? Are there any areas where you are overly *independent?* How does this affect your marital relationship?

2. As a husband are there any areas where you are overly *dependent* on your mother? Your father? Are there any areas where you are overly *independent?* How does this affect your marital relationship?

Parental Maturity

1. As a wife what areas of *maturity* can you identify in your parents? What areas of *immaturity?*

2. As a husband, what areas of *maturity* can you identify in your parents? What areas of *immaturity?*

3. How do these dynamics affect your husband/wife relationships?

Emotional Transference

1. As a wife are there any negative emotions you have experienced toward your parents that you are now transferring to your husband? How does this affect your husband's attitudes and behavior toward you?

2. As a husband are there any negative emotions you have experienced toward your parents that you are now transferring to your wife? How does this affect your wife's attitudes and behavior toward you?

Step 3—Share what you have written (Exercise 5 in *The Measure of a Marriage Workbook*) with your mate. Take turns sharing your answers. Ask each other whether or not you agree with the observations.

Step 4—Write out specific goals (Exercise 6 in *The Measure of a Marriage Notebook*) that relate to specific areas of need in your marriage. The following section, "Overcoming Problems," will illustrate this process.

Overcoming Problems

Isolating problems and understanding their nature is the place to start in solving them. However, you must go a step further. *Insight* is only the beginning. You must set specific goals to overcome these problems. What goals should you set in your marriage in order to help you to maturely "leave father and mother"? The following illustrations will help you in your goal-setting process:

Case 1: Jane has a consistent tendency to talk to her mother every time she feels *insecurity* in her marriage.

Her goal is to sensitively share these feelings with her husband rather than her mother. Jim, her husband, has set up the goal to listen objectively and nondefensively to Jane when she shares these feelings and to do what he can to help her overcome her insecurities.

Case 2: Jim reacts negatively to his wife every time she asks him to do something around the house. His primary goal is to volunteer to do certain things before he is asked. Secondly, his goal is to be emotionally open to his wife's requests—realizing he is subconsciously reacting to his mother. On the other hand, Jane's goal is to ask Jim to do things with a different tone of voice. She realizes she conveys her desires in a rather demanding way. So, she is trying to avoid sounding like Jim's mother.

Case 3: Both Jim and Jane realize that *his* mother tries to control their marriage. They have set up two short-range goals and one long-range goal.

First, Jim is going to talk to his mother openly but sensitively, asking her not to interfere with their marriage. He plans to talk with his father privately, sharing why he is going to talk with his mother.

Second, Jane is simultaneously going to do all she can to let Jim's mother know she really cares about her—sending her a note of appreciation, calling her periodically to carry on a friendly conversation, etc.

Third, if the problem persists, Jim and Jane are considering moving to another part of the city to avoid geographical closeness.

AS A GROUP OF COUPLES: Leader's Instructions
Step 1—Review for the group the biblical material and illustrations in chapter 3. (See pages 34-39.)

Suggestion: Read the illustrations out loud to the class under the three problem areas; that is, (1) developing unhealthy dependence; (2) immature parents; and (3) emotional transference.

Step 2—Divide the men into small groups and the women into small groups. Have each group appoint a leader and recorder/reporter. Then have each group take 15 minutes and discuss the answers to the following questions:

Questions for Husbands

1. What areas in a wife's personality can reflect *over-dependency* on her mother? On her father? How can this negatively affect a marital relationship?

2. What areas in a wife's personality can reflect an overly *independent* attitude toward her mother or father?

3. What areas of immaturity on the part of *in-laws* can create problems in their children's marriage?

4. What possible areas of parental emotional transference are apt to show up in a wife's personality, thus affecting her relationship with her husband? What are the possible negative effects in the marriage?

Questions for Wives

1. What areas in a husband's personality can reflect *over-dependency* on his mother? On his father? How can this negatively affect a marital relationship?

2. What areas in a husband's personality can reflect an overly *independent* attitude toward his mother or father?

3. What areas of immaturity on the part of *in-laws* can create problems in their children's marriage?

4. What possible areas of parental emotional transference are apt to show up in a husband's personality, thus affecting his relationship with his wife? What are the possible negative effects in the marriage?

Step 3—Have the recorders for each men's group report their answers to the whole group. Ask the women to listen carefully. Then have the women recorders report their findings while the men listen carefully.

Note: If your class is small you may have all the group members participate in the reporting.

Couple Assignment

Ask each couple to complete at home the four-step project on pages 50-51 in this book. They should use their copy of *The Measure of a Marriage Workbook* to complete the evaluation scales (Exercises 2,3,4) on "Dependence vs. Independence," "Mature or Immature Parents," and "Emotional Transference," and answer the questions (Exercise 5). Then they should set goals (Exercise 6) for overcoming problems after they have read the case studies on pages 51,52 of this book.

CHAPTER 5

Loving as Christ Loved

If someone were to ask you to identify a person in history who demonstrated true love more than any other individual, what would you say? The fact is that most people who live in our culture, if asked that question, would probably identify that person as Jesus Christ. Even people who have studied His life very little, or who would not be particularly enthused about His teachings or personal claims would still credit Him with being a man who demonstrated supreme love, far beyond any other human being.

Biblical writers—especially Paul the apostle— identify Christ quite frequently as an example of love in human relationships. They particularly uphold Christ's example in the most unique of all human relationships— marriage! But unfortunately, some students of the Bible have attempted to interpret scriptural directives about these marital relationships without considering directives to *all* Christians regarding their overall relationships with one another. This often leads to erroneous conclusions regarding husband and wife roles. And today, these erroneous conclusions are most often reflected by religious leaders who are dispensing simplistic and almost dogmatic solutions to marital conflicts and problems.

It's imperative that we realize that the instructions which the New Testament gives us, particularly in the letters written to various churches in the first-century world, were in the most part written to *all* Christians. It is true, however, that within this larger context there are some specific instructions given to certain individuals within these churches—such as husbands and wives. But if we attempt to isolate instructions directed to these individuals, we will come up with interpretations that are indeed narrow, restrictive, simplistic and in some instances totally unworkable.

Let me illustrate. Often we have zeroed in on Paul's statements in his letters to the Ephesians and Colossians that husbands are to love "as Christ loved" (see Eph. 5:25; Col 3:19), and wives are to "submit to [their] husbands" (see Eph. 5:22; Col. 3:18) without considering the larger context of these statements. Consequently, we have come up with conclusions regarding husband and wife relationships that are in some respects unscriptural and often offensive to those who understand more thoroughly the dynamics of human personality and interpersonal relationships, particularly from a sociological and psychological point of view.

To love "as Christ loved" is probably one of the most foundational directives and principles in all of Scripture.

It was Christ's "new commandment" to the apostles. "Love one another," He said, "even as I have loved you" (John 13:34). It is stated as the greatest mark of maturity among followers of Christ, "But now abide faith, hope, love, these three; but the greatest of these is love. Pursue love" (1 Cor. 13:13; 14:1).

To love is either directly or indirectly given as an imperative in Scripture more than any other directive. And it is the key to unity and harmony in human relationships (see John 17:20-23). By obeying God in this area of our lives, we can fulfill the whole law of God (see Rom. 13:10; Gal. 5:13,14; and Jas. 2:8).

If loving "as Christ loved" is foundational in enabling *all* of us to become one, how much more so in a marital relationship. It certainly provides the broad frame of reference, or to put it another way, it becomes the overarching principle for keeping all other scriptural directives in proper focus.

Focusing on Others

What does it mean to love "as Christ loved"? Perhaps the most graphic illustration is given by Paul in his letter to the Philippians. Initially, Paul gave a specific exhortation: "Do *nothing* out of selfish ambition or vain conceit, but in humility consider others better than yourselves. Each of you should look not only to your own interests, but also to the interests of others" (Phil. 2:3,4 *NIV*).

Just reading this paragraph from Paul's letter makes it quite clear how this directive will affect a marital relationship. The principle of loving "as Christ loved" puts the focus immediately on our partner's needs, not on our own. In *everything* we do, our goal should be to consider the other person's needs and concerns first.

Paul goes on to spell out how Christ demonstrated these attitudes and actions toward us.

First, he said, there's to be an attitude of unselfishness. "Your attitude should be the same as that of Christ Jesus: who, being in very nature God, did not consider equality with God something to be grasped" (Phil. 2:5,6, *NIV*).

In other words, Christ did not cling to His heavenly position with His Father, but was willing to lay it aside to come into this world—the world He made. And in His incarnation He identified with our fallen condition, though He, of course, did not personally participate in sin. He did, however, give up the glories of heaven to live among men. And when He did so He was demonstrating an unselfish attitude that is unparalleled in the universe.

Second, Christ's love was demonstrated by an attitude of humility (see Phil. 2:7). Christ, who was "in very nature God" (v. 6), voluntarily "made himself nothing." He who created all things temporarily laid aside His heavenly glory. He who was and is God took upon Himself "the very nature of a servant." He who made man took upon Himself "human likeness." This, of course, is ultimate humility personified.

Third, Christ demonstrated an attitude of sacrifice and self-giving. His actions illustrate the greatest act of love ever known to mankind. "Being found in appearance as a man, he humbled himself and became obedient to death—even death on a cross!" (Phil. 2:8, *NIV*). Jesus Christ died that we might live eternally. Because man's sin demanded the penalty of death, Jesus Christ died for every man, even His enemies. Thus, when they nailed Him to the cross, He prayed, "Father, forgive them, for they do not know what they are doing" (Luke 23:34, *NIV*).

Paul wrote these words in Philippians to all Christians who are supposed to emulate Christ in their relationships with others. But it is also a powerful demonstration and elaboration for both husbands and wives of what it means to love "as Christ loved."

Focusing on Husbands

Why did Paul zero in on husbands when a wife is also to love "as Christ loved"? The answer is clear when we understand the specific temptation that most men face—the temptation to focus on their own needs and to "use" women selfishly. This was particularly true in the first-century world. Culturally, women were commonly treated like slaves and second-class citizens. These men, converted to Christianity out of a pagan life-style, needed to be told what their proper attitude toward their wives was to be.

But it is also true that men in *all* cultures and in any given moment in history need this emphasis. There is within men a tendency toward selfishness that seems to be uniquely male. This is particularly true in the area of sex. It is very easy to be naturally demanding, insensitive, selfish and manipulative. Paul—a man—knew that. Consequently, he bore down on this injunction for husbands.

Furthermore, the very authority and responsibility God has given husbands makes this emphasis necessary. *First, like Christ, they are to have an attitude of unselfishness*. Like Jesus, a Christian husband should not grasp and hold on to his position of authority, using it as a manipulative device to get what he wants. True, there may be times when he must make decisions and judgments that will cause a certain amount of resistance and even emotional pain, but he must always use the authority for the benefit of his mate. Whatever he does must be done to protect his wife and to assist her in her personal growth. Christ's goal for the church is to "make her holy, . . . to present her to himself as a radiant church, without stain or wrinkle or any other blemish, but holy and blameless. In this same way," continued Paul, "husbands ought to love their wives as their own bodies. He who loves his wife loves himself" (Eph. 5:26-28, *NIV*).

Second, a husband, like Christ, should have an attitude of humility. Though God has given man a position of headship and authority, he must realize that he is also a servant. He must never lord it over his wife, using his male ego as an excuse for insensitivity and personal defensiveness that is purely self-protection.

Furthermore, he must identify with his wife—her pain, her heartaches, her struggles, her weaknesses, her anxieties, her stresses, her needs, as well as her joys, her successes, her achievements. Remember that Christ's love caused Him to identify with us. To love our wives as Christ loved the church means physiological, psychological and spiritual identification with them.

Third, a husband who loves "as Christ loved" must demonstrate an attitude of sacrifice and self-giving. This is one of the most difficult facets of Paul's teaching. When it comes to sacrifice, most of us, men and women, operate at a very superficial level. Much of what we do, if we're not careful, is for ourselves. It may appear on the surface to be for the benefit for our mate, but a closer look into the depths of our psychological nature often reveals a selfish person. But the challenge is still there. Though we are imperfect human beings, we must set as our goal pure motives—to love as Christ loved—demonstrating a sacrificial and self-giving spirit.

CHAPTER 6

An Exercise in True Loving

To love "as Christ loved" is probably one of the most difficult challenges facing any couple. It calls for attitudes and actions that run contrary to our natural inclinations. It is much easier for most of us to receive than to give; to be self-centered than to focus on others; to be ministered unto than to minister. And indeed we must be able to receive, to have our share of attention and to be ministered unto. But to focus on ourselves primarily destroys that unique process that *must* put others first if we are to follow Christ's example. The following exercise will help you develop these qualities in your own life first—and then in your marriage.

AS AN INDIVIDUAL

Evaluate your relationship with your mate in light of

Christ's example of unselfishness, humility and sacrifice and self-giving. The following evaluation scales will assist you in this process.

Note: It is true that there are circumstances making some of the following attitudes and actions appropriate and essential. But generally, these statements represent behavior that is basically selfish, proud and unsacrificial. In short, they do not reflect Christ's example of love.

A Quiz for Husbands

Instructions: Circle the T to indicate that you feel the statement is *mostly* true regarding your behavior. Circle the F to indicate the statement is *mostly* false regarding your behavior.

☐ 1. When I come home from work I immediately seek a place of privacy where I can do my own thing.   T   F

☐ 2. When I come home from work I want my wife to be available immediately to listen to my problems.   T   F

☐ 3. I resent it when my wife is running behind schedule with her meal preparation.   T   F

☐ 4. I do not expect to help with the children when I'm home.   T   F

☐ 5. I seldom think about the burden my wife carries when she is home all day with the children.   T   F

☐ 6. When I want to have sexual relations with my wife, I seldom think about her personal schedule.   T   F

☐ 7. I resent it when my wife gets attention.   T   F

☐ 8. I seldom thank my wife for cooking meals and taking care of the home.   T   F

☐ 9. I seldom suggest to my wife that we eat out.   T   F

☐ 10. I resent it when my wife sleeps late in the morning.   T   F

☐ 11. I resent it when my wife stays up late to get things done around the house.   T   F

☐ 12. I seldom ask my wife what I can do to help her with her work.   T   F

☐ 13. When I have a day off I usually plan to spend it with my male companions. (Golfing, playing tennis, etc.)   T   F

☐ 14. When I have a choice between spending time with my wife and my friends, I usually choose to spend time with my friends.   T   F

☐ 15. When I have a choice between spending time with my wife or my children, I usually spend time with my children.   T   F

☐ 16. I seldom call my wife during the day and tell her I miss her and love her.   T   F

☐ 17. I seldom think about how to encourage my wife when I come home from work.   T   F

☐ 18. I seldom think about my wife's personal needs.   T   F

☐ 19. I seldom think about how to be a creative lover.   T   F

☐ 20. I expect my wife to initiate sexual relations.   T   F

☐ 21. I seldom think about my wife during the day.   T   F

☐ 22. I seldom make an effort to know what   T F
my wife is doing during the day; that
is, to become aware of her personal
work schedule.

☐ 23. I'd rather spend most of my time by   T F
myself.

☐ 24. When I know I'm going to be coming   T F
home later than normal I usually do not
call my wife to explain.

☐ 25. I seldom ask my wife for permission to   T F
do things.

☐ 26. I resent having to spend money on my   T F
wife.

☐ 27. If I had it to do over again, I'd rather   T F
not have children.

☐ 28. I seldom express appreciation to my   T F
wife for her ministry to me and my
children.

☐ 29. I resent having to work to earn a living   T F
for my family.

☐ 30. I seldom postpone my desire for sexual   T F
activities.

☐ 31. I seldom spend time preparing my wife   T F
emotionally for our sexual experience
or helping her reach a sexual climax.

☐ 32. I seldom write love notes to my   T F
wife.

☐ 33. Most of the time when I say, "I love   T F
you," is when I'm having sexual relations with my wife.

☐ 34. I resent the children's demands upon   T F
my wife when I want to spend time
with her privately.

A Quiz for Wives

Instructions: Circle the T to indicate you feel the statement is *mostly* true regarding your behavior. Circle the F to indicate the statement is *mostly* false.

☐ 1. When my husband comes home from work I immediately ask him to sit down and listen to my problems.   T   F

☐ 2. When I see my husband has a few spare moments at home I present him with a list of things that I want him to do around the house.   T   F

☐ 3. I resent it when my husband sits down in the family room and watches television—especially when I'm preparing the meal.   T   F

☐ 4. I expect my husband to take care of the children while he's home.   T   F

☐ 5. I resent the fact that my husband is away from the children during the day and I have to take care of them.   T   F

☐ 6. I find myself quite frequently emotionally resistant when I know my husband has sexual interests and needs.   T   F

☐ 7. I resent the fact that my husband gets more attention from others than I do.   T   F

☐ 8. I resent having to cook meals and take care of the home.   T   F

☐ 9. I want to eat out most of the time.   T   F

☐ 10. I sleep late most days, getting up after my husband leaves for work.   T   F

☐ 11. I usually stay up late to do things after my husband goes to bed.   T   F

☐ 12. I seldom ask my husband what I can do   T   F
to help him with his work.

☐ 13. I spend more time with my friends than   T   F
with my husband.

☐ 14. When I have a choice between setting   T   F
aside time to be with my husband or
my friends I usually set aside time to be
with my friends.

☐ 15. When I have a choice between setting   T   F
aside time to be with my husband or
my children I usually set aside time to
be with my children.

☐ 16. I seldom call my husband at work and   T   F
tell him I miss him and love him.

☐ 17. I seldom plan how I can make my   T   F
husband feel welcome when he comes
home from work.

☐ 18. I seldom think about my husband's   T   F
personal needs.

☐ 19. I seldom think about how to be a crea-   T   F
tive lover.

☐ 20. I seldom initiate sexual relations.   T   F

☐ 21. I seldom think about my husband dur-   T   F
ing the day when he's not home.

☐ 22. I seldom make an effort to know what   T   F
my husband is doing during the day;
that is, his personal work schedule.

☐ 23. I'd rather spend most of my time by   T   F
myself.

☐ 24. If I'm going to be gone when my   T   F
husband comes home, I usually do not
leave a note or call him and explain
changes in my personal scheduling.

☐ 25. I seldom ask my husband's permission to do things.   T   F

☐ 26. I resent the fact that I don't have a separate bank account.   T   F

☐ 27. If I had it to do over again, I'd rather not have children.   T   F

☐ 28. I seldom thank my husband for his commitment to his job and for providing materially for my personal needs.   T   F

☐ 29. I resent having to care for the children, keep up the home, prepare meals, etc.   T   F

☐ 30. I resent my husband's sexual requests.   T   F

☐ 31. I resent the fact that my husband is fulfilled sexually.   T   F

☐ 32. I seldom write love notes to my husband.   T   F

☐ 33. I seldom tell my husband how much I love him.   T   F

☐ 34. I resent the children's demands upon my husband when I want to spend time with him privately.   T   F

Having worked through the particular scale designed for you, go back over your T and F responses. Wherever you find a T, put a check (✔) in the box provided at the beginning of each item. These checks will identify areas that *may* (but not always) represent areas of selfish and unloving attitudes and actions on your part in your relationship with your mate. Use these areas to write out some specific goals that you want to achieve that will cause you to love more as Christ loved! Hopefully, this will help your mate to reciprocate.

Note: If your mate is open to making this a reciprocal

process, move on to the couple project and work through the evaluation scales together.

AS A COUPLE

Step 1—As a husband and wife, complete the evaluation scales designed for each of you, Exercise 7 in *The Measure of a Marriage Workbook*.

Step 2—Now that you've completed the evaluation scales designed for each of you, fill out the one designed to evaluate your mate, Exercise 8 in *The Measure of a Marriage Workbook*.

Step 3—Compare your evaluation of your mate (Exercise 8) with your mate's self-evaluation (Exercise 7). To isolate areas of discrepancy as well as areas of agreement, record your answers and your mate's answers in Exercise 9, in *The Measure of a Marriage Workbook*, which is designed for a comparative study.

Step 4—Now that you have recorded your answers on the forms designed for a comparative study, isolate the areas of discrepancy by placing a check (✔) in the box provided before each statement in Exercise 9. Then discuss the areas of discrepancy and why you think they exist. Do so as sensitively and as nondefensively as possible.

Step 5—Following your discussion of the comparative study, each of you should go through the *original* evaluation scale, Exercise 7, designed for each of you and place a check (✔) in the box provided by each item which you marked T for mostly true about yourselves.

Note: Answers you've marked T about yourselves indicate areas of life that usually (but not always) focus on oneself rather than the other partner. Utilizing your observations from both the comparative studies as well as your personal scales, set up personal goals for your marriage.

Caution: Each marital partner is entitled to his own rights in a marriage. To say we have no rights is an oversimplification. For example, a wife needs a husband who will sit down and listen to her problems; also, a husband needs the same attention. However, if we consistently demand this right, we have put the primary focus on ourselves rather than on our mate. To do so, violates Jesus' example who came to "minister" rather than to be "ministered unto." God's will is that both mates reach out to the other to meet each other's needs. When we do so, our own needs will be met. The relationship is then in proper focus.

Step 6—Utilizing the observations you've both made as a result of the foregoing process, write out specific goals for yourselves as marital partners. (Exercise 10 in *The Measure of a Marriage Workbook*.)

AS A GROUP OF COUPLES

First, review with the group the biblical material presented in chapter 5. Then divide up into small groups with men and women in separate groups. You may wish to maintain the same groups from session to session. Feel free, however, to mix them up if you feel this is necessary.

Step 1—Have each group of women read through the evaluation items for wives on pages 29-30 in the Workbook and put a check (✔) in the box provided if they feel this is a problem area for the *average* woman. In other words, have them check the item where the average wife would probably have to admit this particular item is "mostly true." Have the men's group go through the same process for their own scale on pages 31,32 in the Workbook.

Step 2—Have each group work through their evaluation scale, noting the checked items and make a statement on a separate sheet of paper as to *why* they believe that is a particular problem for the *average* wife or husband. Appoint a recorder to list the statements.

Step 3—Have each group briefly report their observations. Hear first from the women. Ask the men to listen carefully and as objectively as possible. Then give them a brief period of time to voice their opinions as to whether or not they feel the women are making valid observations.

Then repeat the same process for the men. First have them report and then have the women respond to what they hear.

Note: If you have several groups, ask reporters not to repeat observations another group has shared.

Couple Assignments

Assign couples to complete Exercises 7—10 in *The Measure of a Marriage Workbook*. This time they will use the "mostly true" or "mostly false" approach as it applies to their own marriage.

A Final Thought

All people everywhere have the *potential* to love as Christ loved. But all cannot satisfactorily practice this kind of life-style in their marriages or in any other relationships without knowing personally the One who exemplified this kind of sacrificial love.

This implies more than simply trying to follow His

example. It means coming to know Jesus Christ in a personal way as Saviour and Lord. It is then that He will help each of us love as He loved.

Do you know Christ personally? Have you received Him as your Saviour from sin? If not, you can. Sincerely take the following steps and you will add a dimension to your marriage that you have never known before.

Step 1—Acknowledge before God that you have sinned—that is, you have fallen short of God's divine standard (see Rom. 3:23).

Step 2—Accept the fact that Jesus Christ offered Himself for your sins on the cross and paid the supreme penalty for sin—death (see Rom. 6:23). Believe also that He arose from the dead and because He lives, you too can live eternally with Him.

Step 3—Receive Jesus Christ as your personal Saviour from sin; that is, believe that He not only died and rose again for the sins of the world, but that He died and rose for you (see John 1:12; Rom. 5:1).

Step 4—Confess Jesus Christ before others; that is, let someone know what steps you have taken (see Rom. 10:9,10). Above all, begin to demonstrate with your life-style that you are a follower of Jesus Christ. The best place to begin is in your marital relationship as you begin more than ever before to love "as Christ loved."

CHAPTER 7

Submitting to Each Other

No aspect of marriage has been given more universal attention than wifely submission. And of course it is a very controversial subject at this juncture in our present-day cultural journey—particularly among those who classify themselves as feminists or at least are sympathetic to feminist ideology.

The very word "submission" is threatening. One reason is that we haven't understood its meaning as we should. We sometimes think of submission as allowing another person to dominate and control us. And all of us resist that kind of relationship.

In God's scheme of things, the concept of submission was never to be applicable to only one person in a given relationship. It was to be reciprocal and mutual.

It must be added that there are times when a marital partner (or a person generally) may need to submit under conditions that are not reciprocal. But God never intended this to be the normal rule for any human being, particularly since Christ came and introduced a whole new way of life.

What the Bible Says

The fact is that the Bible *does* teach submission, but not only for wives. It is a quality of life that should characterize *all* of us in our relationships with others. Thus, Paul, before exhorting wives to be submissive to their husbands (see Eph 5:22), exhorted *all* believers to be "subject [to submit] to one another in the fear of Christ" (Eph 5:21).

It's interesting that Paul did not use the word "submission" in his statement to wives. Rather, he based his directive for wives to "submit" on his use of the word in verse 21 when he was speaking to all the followers of Christ in Ephesus. In other words, Paul told all of these people they were to *submit* to one another (Eph. 5:21)— which, he said, includes wives to husbands (5:22), husbands to wives (5:25), children to parents (6:1), fathers to children (6:4), servants to masters (6:5) and masters to servants (6:9). Put another way, Paul's statement to "submit to one another" in verse 21 is the basic concept on which he builds his specific exhortations to the other people mentioned in the remaining part of his Ephesian letter.

That Paul believed that husbands should submit to their wives is clearly illustrated in the fact that they are to love as Christ loved. As we've already seen from Philippians, Christ demonstrated His love by becoming a *servant*, and it is impossible to be a servant without being submissive. Inherent then in Paul's statement to love "as

Christ loved'' is a submissive attitude and spirit.

Why, then, does Paul specifically direct wives to be submissive to their husbands? The answer is that it is not in God's will for a wife to dominate, control or manipulate her husband. In fact, it is not within God's will for *any* Christian to dominate, control or manipulate any other human being. You see, the opposite of submission is control, resistance, domination. There's really no in-between. Either we are submissive, or we are non-submissive. There is, practically speaking, no neutral ground. Either we are teachable, willing to listen to someone else's advice and correction and willing to put the other person first, or we are resistant, unwilling to listen to another person's advice and correction and unwilling to put the other person first. Even a neutral attitude usually represents passive resistance, which is the opposite of having a submissive spirit.

Don't misunderstand! Discussion and dialogue and even disagreement are not necessarily synonymous with a non-submissive attitude. It depends on *how* it is done. Those who classify *all* resistance as non-submissive do not understand the communication process. God forbid that a man never allows his wife to disagree with him. If he does he, at that moment, also becomes non-submissive and certainly is not loving "as Christ loved." Unfortunately, some husbands have interpreted Paul's injunction to wives in this narrow way—which is incorrect and quite frequently rooted in personal pride and insecurity. In short, it reflects a male ego that has not been brought into conformity with Christ's example of love and way of life.

A Larger Perspective

Some theological, historical and cultural background

will help clarify further why Paul emphasized submission for women generally and wives particularly. First, God created Eve for Adam. She was *not* to be his subordinate but his equal. However, when sin entered the world, Eve (and all women following her) had to bear a special burden because Eve was first deceived (see 1 Tim. 2:13,14). If we are to accept the biblical account at all we cannot deny these facts. This is not just merely a Pauline interpretation but rather this concept can be traced all the way through the Bible. Furthermore, history verifies this reality.

However, with the coming of Jesus Christ something unique happened regarding a woman's role. As Christians, a man and wife have the potential to experience a unity and oneness that can grow constantly deeper and more meaningful day by day. From God's eternal and spiritual perspective, there's total equality (see Gal. 3:28). But since marriage is not an eternal relationship and is limited to time and space, man was appointed to be the head (as Christ is the head of the church) and the woman is to recognize his God-given authority. Becoming Christians does not eradicate sin. But in Christ, if a husband and wife continually love each other as Christ loved them, and regularly fulfill their God-ordained responsibilities and trust each other, they have the potential to experience a growing unity and oneness that can actually be a foretaste of heaven on this side of glory. Have you experienced some of this unity in your marriage?

A Psychological Reaction

In the New Testament world Paul had to deal with the problem of women who, once set free from the demands of their pagan religions, began to use their freedom in irresponsible ways. Naturally, the first area where it would be most observable would be in their relationships with their husbands. Having been put down for years and treated like slaves, they found themselves now with the opportunity for dominance and control.

This we ought to understand. Any group of people who has been mistreated and kept in bondage, once set free, will normally overreact. People like this often do not know *how* to handle this freedom.

This has been obvious in our own culture. Some minority groups have had to learn to handle freedom since for years they were mistreated, kept ignorant and in bondage. It takes time to overcome these social restrictions and our tendencies to overreact.

Some women today who are experiencing new freedom are likewise overreacting. For years in *our* culture many women have been mistreated. In the non-Christian world particularly, men have been notorious for using women for their own ends. On the current scene we see the "Playboy philosophy" that views women as toys, as playthings, as a means to selfish pleasure. It is no wonder that most thinking women react against this self-centered philosophy. Today, more than ever before, women are used for materialistic purposes. Sex sells anything, and women of course are the primary targets for this abuse. Again, it should not be surprising that many women react against such selfish exploitation.

Women also react to the general male selfishness that permeates the whole society in which we live. They have often been treated as inferior personalities, incapable of certain roles. They've often been kept "in their place" primarily because men have been threatened by the women's abilities. Again, it should not surprise us that women can see through such egocentric behavior.

But where can these women turn? What is their source of authority for what they do? Unfortunately, many do not have or they reject any divine perspective. Motivated by the same sinful nature that motivates men, they are seeking liberation without God's principles. They do not realize that without Jesus Christ's attitudes they can never know true freedom. Consequently, they overreact, moving first in one direction and then in another. Being non-submissive certainly will not set them free any more than it sets a man free. No wonder the world is filled with frustrated people, many sincerely trying but never coming to a knowledge of these principles and the secret to what they are looking for.

The only answer to this overreaction is to follow Christ's example and instructions. Then husbands can love their wives as Christ loved the church—which includes submission. And wives can submit to their husbands as the church is subject to Christ—which certainly includes loving ''as Christ loved.'' In fact, Christ's love is the basis for mutual submission. And mutual submission is possible without eliminating the husband's ''headship.'' Applying these biblical principles is the *only* way to experience *functional* egalitarianism and still maintain the husband/wife roles specified in Scripture.

CHAPTER 8

An Exercise in Submitting

Marriage, more than any other relationship, includes many areas calling for mutual submission. What are these areas? To what extent are you submissive? Why are you having difficulty submitting? In what ways do you make it difficult for your mate to submit to you? How can you become a more submissive person?

This chapter is designed to help you answer these questions.

AS AN INDIVIDUAL

Following is a list of those areas in marriage that commonly create difficulty in submitting to each other. There's also room to add any that are not listed but are problem areas for you.

Step 1—Circle the number in the scale following each item to indicate the degree to which there is a problem in submitting to your mate. If it is *never* a problem circle number 1; if it is *always* a problem, circle number 7; or, circle any number between 1 and 7 that indicates the degree to which you have trouble in submitting to your mate in your marriage.

I find it difficult to submit when:	*Never a Problem*				*Always a Problem*		
☐ 1. My mate asks me to do things that are routine and boring;	1	2	3	4	5	6	7
☐ 2. My mate asks me to be more frugal in spending money;	1	2	3	4	5	6	7
☐ 3. My mate asks me to be more neat in personal grooming;	1	2	3	4	5	6	7
☐ 4. My mate asks me directly or indirectly to meet sexual needs;	1	2	3	4	5	6	7
☐ 5. My mate asks me to break a personal habit;	1	2	3	4	5	6	7
☐ 6. My mate asks me to be more orderly in my personal life;	1	2	3	4	5	6	7
☐ 7. My mate asks me to give up something I plan to do in order to do something my mate wants to do;	1	2	3	4	5	6	7

		Never a Problem				Always a Problem		
☐	8. My mate asks me to set goals for my life and family;	1	2	3	4	5	6	7
☐	9. My mate asks for a period of time to communicate;	1	2	3	4	5	6	7
☐	10. My mate asks me to do something immediately when I plan to do it later;	1	2	3	4	5	6	7
☐	11. My mate asks me to do something I usually do anyway;	1	2	3	4	5	6	7
☐	12. My mate asks me directly or indirectly to be more creative in our lovemaking;	1	2	3	4	5	6	7
☐	13. My mate asks me to do something I feel is my mate's responsibility;	1	2	3	4	5	6	7
☐	14. My mate asks me to help with the children;	1	2	3	4	5	6	7
☐	15. My mate asks me to help with his or her work;	1	2	3	4	5	6	7
☐	16. My mate asks me to explain my personal schedule;	1	2	3	4	5	6	7
☐	17. Other _____	1	2	3	4	5	6	7

Step 2—Now that you have indicated the degree to which this is a problem in submitting to your mate, go through the items again and print an initial in the box provided at the beginning of each statement to indicate who you feel is primarily at fault. If you feel it is primarily your husband's fault that you have difficulty submitting to him, print an H in the box. If you feel it is primarily your wife's fault that you have difficulty submitting to her, print a W in the box. If you feel the fault is about evenly divided, print a B in the box.

Remember: Marriage is a two-way street. You may have difficulties submitting because of your partner's attitudes and behavior. On the other hand, you may be as much or more to blame than your mate.

Step 3—Sit down with a close friend of the same sex who is mature, happily married, and who is aware of your marital relationship and who will not favor your point of view just because he or she is your close friend. Ask your friend to evaluate your answers and to indicate the extent to which he or she thinks you have been objective in your responses. Also, seek your friend's advice as to *why* you may be having difficulties in certain areas of your relationship.

Note: If your friend believes that the problem is mostly your mate's, you may need to seek counsel from your pastor or some other competent marriage counselor. If your friend indicates it appears to be mostly your own attitudes and behavior, you may be able to handle the problem with your friend's advice, help and support. If not, do not hesitate to seek counsel from someone who specializes in helping people overcome marriage problems.

AS A COUPLE

Step 1—As a husband and wife, complete the "Submission Scale for Husbands" and the "Submission Scale for Wives" (Exercise 11) in *The Measure of a Marriage Workbook*.

Step 2—After evaluating yourself in terms of submission, evaluate *each other*. Complete the two scales in Exercise 12.

Step 3—Now that you have evaluated yourself personally as well as each other, compare your answers. To do this, fill in the blanks by each item on the comparative forms (Exercise 13).

Step 4—Compare your answers by placing a check in the box provided by each item in the scale, Exercise 13, where there are two or more points of difference in your evaluations. Then discuss with each other why you believe this variance exists. Take turns sharing and listening to each other. Discuss together as objectively as possible how you can help each other more easily submit to each other's desires.

Note: If you cannot work through this project satisfactorily, arriving at a degree of mutual understanding and concern for each other, you no doubt need to seek help from a professional marriage counselor. The sooner you do so, the better.

Step 5—Write out several personal goals that result from your discussion (Exercise 14).

AS A GROUP OF COUPLES

Step 1—Pass out sheets of paper and ask each individual to anonymously record *three* areas in his or her

marriage that present the greatest difficulty in being submissive to the other marital partner.

Note: Ask each person to identify at the top of the
sheet whether he/she is a husband or a wife.

Step 2—Collect the answer sheets. As a group leader,
share what the wives have recorded and then share what
the husbands have recorded.

Note: Ask a woman to record the results of the wives
reports and a man to record the results of the husbands
report. Ask each recorder to tabulate the number of times
an area of difficulty is repeated.

Step 3—As previously, divide the total group into
smaller groups (men with men and women with women).
Each group should select a leader and recorder and then
answer two questions regarding the two areas of difficulty
that were mentioned the most. The questions are:

1. *Why* is this a problem?
2. *What* can be done specifically to overcome these
problems?

Note: This process will take at least 10 minutes.

Step 4—Have each group recorder report the results of
each group's discussion.

Note: Ask each recorder to avoid repetition in their
reports.

Couple Assignments

Complete the project for couples outlined in this text,
using Exercises 11,12,13 and 14 in *The Measure of a
Marriage Workbook.*

CHAPTER 9

Learning to Love

A couple I knew were having serious problems in their marriage. One of the pastors in our church met with the husband one day for lunch and very pointedly asked him if he loved his wife.

"Yes," he responded, "I love her."

"May I read something to you?" asked the pastor. He opened his Bible and read from 1 Corinthians 13, which outlines the qualities which Paul defined as love:

- Love is patient
- Love is kind
- Love does not envy
- Love does not boast
- Love is not proud
- Love is not rude
- Love is not self-seeking

- Love is not easily angered
- Love keeps no record of wrongs
- Love does not delight in evil
- Love rejoices in the truth
- Love always protects
- Love always trusts
- Love always hopes
- Love always perseveres.

After the pastor had read this list from 1 Corinthians 13:4-8, he asked the question again: "Do you really love your wife?"

Without a moment's hesitation the husband responded: "No, I really don't love my wife—not that way!"

You see, the man's first response was based on our contemporary culture's definition of love—often primarily sexual feelings. And in this case, which can be multiplied again and again, what this man defined as "love" was probably not love at all.

Unfortunately, our Western culture particularly has propagated the idea that *feelings* of attraction and particularly *sexual* feelings are the essence of love. This is a very superficial and inadequate explanation of what keeps a marital relationship on track. In many instances what is initially classified as "love" is a *selfish* feeling—a *desire* to have the other person satisfy a personal need.

Let's look at another example. Tom and Diane were intensely attracted to each other during their dating and courtship experience. They were so emotionally involved that they engaged in various kinds of sexual activity. Both of them felt guilty about their behavior, but it didn't seem to diminish their "feelings" for each other, so they continued to be intimate prior to marriage.

Shortly after they were officially married, something began to happen. They discovered that living together 24 hours a day was quite different from seeing each other several times a week. They became aware very quickly that marriage involves far more than dinner out, dim lights, quiet music and a carefree evening together. In fact, Diane's attitude toward sexual involvement changed, which confused her and Tom. Right now both are going through a state of disillusionment. Unknown to both of them, neither has really learned to love each other.

More than ever before we need a more adequate view of premarital and marital love. I believe the Bible provides that view. There is no other source that provides a better perspective. All other approaches are limited, unsatisfactory and ultimately disillusioning.

Agape Love

The words *agapao* and *agape* are used most frequently in the New Testament to describe love. In most instances these Greek words are used to portray loving acts—that is, behaving in certain ways because it is the *right thing* to do. Though *agape* love should normally be combined with positive feelings, it is the kind of love that should cause me to meet my mate's needs, no matter how I personally feel about it.

Jesus Christ demonstrated this love dramatically when He voluntarily suffered on the cross, even though, at the *feeling level,* His *human* desire was to escape the agony that lay before Him. In spite of His painful ambivalence He did what He totally believed was the will of God.

Experience bears out why this kind of love *must* form the foundation for every marriage. If we performed our responsibilities to each other only when we *felt* like it, we would frequently leave undone many important things that contribute to marital harmony. For example, a man who faces a really tough day in the office in order to earn money to provide for his family does not always—at least at that moment—attack his responsibilities with strong motivation and positive emotions. But, *if* he really behaves toward his wife and family as Christ loved him, he'll do what is right, in spite of his negative feelings.

The same is true of wives and mothers. Washing clothes, preparing meals, and cleaning the house are not always the most exciting responsibilities. And it is even less exciting for a husband to lend a helping hand when he has just faced a day at the office that has been difficult and draining. And when a husband asks his wife—who has had a difficult day at home—for help with some of his office work, her own emotions don't usually cry out with anticipation to cooperate.

Husbands and wives who are mature intellectually *know* there are difficult moments in marriage. And because they are mature psychologically and spiritually, their love for each other ultimately transcends their selfish tendencies. They often perform responsibilities for each other in spite of their negative feelings. In fact, meeting the needs of each other in times like these is the fastest way to "feel good" about ourselves and our marital role.

On the other hand, *agape* love also causes husbands and wives to be sensitive to each other's emotional moods. There are times when the most loving thing to do is not to place demands on our mates. And, at the same time, the most loving thing to do in response may mean not taking advantage of our mate's willingness to forego a need, be it emotional, social, spiritual or physical. Men and women who indeed love according to God's perspective and Christ's example are able to work through these situations with sensitivity, maturity and good balance. They're very much aware that marital life is not always a rose garden.

Phileo Love

The Greek word *phileo* is often used interchangeably in the New Testament with *agapao,* but seemingly is also used distinctively to refer to love that is emotionally positive in nature. It is associated with true friendship. It involves delight and pleasure in doing something. Perhaps one of the best definitions of this kind of love is "a deep emotional feeling of trust generated from one person to another person."[1]

This is the kind of love Paul is referring to in Romans 12:10 when he writes: "Be devoted to one another in *brotherly love.*" The Greek word translated "brotherly love" is *philadelphia.* It involves the idea of *phileo* love toward family members. But in this context Paul was using the kind of loving relationships that should exist among family members to illustrate the kind of relationships that should also exist among members of God's family.

In Christ, husbands and wives are also brothers and sisters. They too are to "be devoted to one another in brotherly love." And this is a special kind of love. Paul made this clear when he used the phrase "be devoted," which literally refers to the mutual affection that should exist between husbands and wives as well as other family members. Consequently, the *King James Version* reads, "Be kindly *affectioned* one to another in brotherly love," and Beck translates, "Love one another *tenderly* as fellow Christians."

This leads to a very important observation. The Bible uses different words to describe love. Though they are not always mutually exclusive in meaning, there are some important distinctions that relate to the subject before us—learning to love.

This distinction seems to be most clearly seen in Paul's instructions to women in Titus 2:3,4. "Likewise," Paul wrote, "teach the older women" and "then they can train the younger women *to love their husbands*" (*NIV*). This phrase is translated from the basic Greek word *philandros*.

Note that Paul assumes in these instructions to women in his letter to Titus that *phileo* love can be learned. In other words, we can engage not only in proper behavior toward our mate, but also develop positive feelings, particularly when we have positive models in other people.

Erao Love

There's another word for "love" that was used by Greek-speaking people in the first century—the word *erao*. Usually it referred to sexual love. Interestingly, this word is never used by New Testament authors. This does not mean that sexual love is wrong or improper, or is never referred to in the New Testament. However, biblical writers no doubt avoided this word because it was so frequently used in their culture to describe illicit sexual activity. Though it is not totally an accurate comparison, there are certain words for sexual expressions in our present-day culture that we avoid in most proper public discussions of sexual love. Though these words are frequently used by people to describe and talk about illicit sex in literature, movies and jokes, they're considered unacceptable, particularly by those who consider sex sacred.

Erotic experience, nevertheless, is an important part of marital love. Without it, marriage can never be what God intended it to be. It's that dimension of our personalities that enables a man and woman to be emotionally attracted to each other in ways that go beyond feelings of friendship. It enables a husband and wife to enjoy each other at levels of communication that are biblically off limits among men and women generally and family members particularly.

This does not mean that erotic feelings will not emerge under certain conditions leading to improper sexual behavior. The same human capacities that are designed by God to be used properly sometimes lead to premarital sexual activity, extramarital affairs, homosexual relationships and even incest. The important point is that when a man or woman engages in erotic lovemaking, they do so according to God's will. They should avoid conditions that lead to illicit sexual behavior. And if, on occasion, sexual feelings emerge (which in themselves are not wrong), they should avoid the inappropriate mental and physical actions that can easily follow.

As stated earlier, our present culture often defines love in emotional and sexual terms. For example, the words of most popular songs that speak of male and female relationships are clearly focused on sexual feelings. The theme of most movies, books and magazines that feature relationships between men and women also focus on this kind of love. Consequently, when a man says to a woman, "I love you," and the woman says, "I love you, too," the essence of their feelings at that moment are frequently sexual. And more recently in our own culture this kind of definition of love is openly featured in homosexual relationships.

This confuses many people, both men and women, old and young, married and unmarried. This was Tom and Diane's problem who were mentioned earlier. Victims of the twentieth-century culture, they thought they were in love. To a certain extent they may have been, but actually their relationship was based primarily on sexual or erotic feelings which God designed to be a vital and legitimate part of *agape* and *phileo* love. But in their case, sexual feelings were operative in a context void of a mature understanding of love that keeps the ebb and flow of erotic feelings from causing disillusionment and confusion. To keep their marriage intact they only had one choice. They must now really learn to love each other.

A Total Perspective

The Scriptures present the concept of love as three-dimensional. In its broadest meaning it involves attitudes and actions that are right and proper, no matter how we feel (see fig. 1, p. 94). *Agapao* love rises above feelings that may be more negative than positive. As previously stated, this is the kind of love Jesus Christ demonstrated when He with an act of His will chose the cross. In His humanity He agonized over this decision. He actually prayed that He might be released from the suffering that lay ahead (see Luke 22:42). However, He knew what His Father's will was and He died on the cross, though every ounce of human emotion within His being cried out for deliverance. He willingly gave up His life for others.

This is the ultimate in *agape* love. And it is God's will for all Christians in *all* relationships to "live a life of love, just as Christ loved us and gave himself up for us as a fragrant offering and sacrifice to God'' (Eph. 5:2, *NIV*). This particularly applies to marriage partners.

Phileo love involves positive feelings and should always be a part of and guided by *agape* love (see fig. 1, p. 94). In fact, it is *agape* love that keeps feelings of affection from becoming selfish and demanding. Many friendships have been destroyed by people who try to keep a relationship purely to themselves.

This also happens in marriage. Both husbands and wives need friendships with other men and women. A jealous spouse can literally destroy and crush a relationship, turning it into a nightmare of emotional pain. On the other hand, marital partners who indeed love according to God's standards, will never allow friendships outside the marriage to interfere with their own marriage. Mature Christians who are guided by *agape* love, as it is defined in the Bible, will maintain this intricate balance.

Erotic feelings and actions are also a part of the circle of biblical love. *Erao* love has been designed by God to be used and enjoyed fully, but it is always to be expressed within the boundaries of *agapao* and *phileo* love (see fig. 1, p. 94). It is this larger context that keeps a relationship morally on track. And it is only this larger context that will keep these feelings from being used in purely selfish ways, even in a marital relationship. Furthermore, it is this larger context that helps a married couple keep their emotional equilibrium during the many times when married life is difficult and demanding.

Note

1. Mort Katz, *Marriage Survival Kit* (Rockville Centre, NY: Farnsworth Publishing Company, Inc., 1974), p. 44.

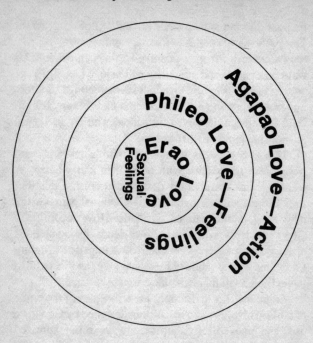

**THE CIRCLE OF
BIBLICAL LOVE**

Doing what is right and best for someone, even if it involves negative feelings.

Responding to someone's needs affectionately and with positive emotions, but always within the guidelines of *agape* love.

Becoming both emotionally and physically involved with another person sexually, but always within the guidelines of *agape* and *phileo* love.

Figure 1

CHAPTER 10

An Exercise in Developing Action Love

There is no simple formula for learning to love another person in a total sense. First of all, it requires being obedient to God (see John 15:10-12) and many times that is a difficult assignment emotionally.

First Corinthians 13 probably outlines the dimensions of *agape* love more completely than any other passage of Scripture. The scale on page 96 will help you measure your growth in expressing *agape* love toward your mate.

AS AN INDIVIDUAL

In the exercise on page 96, indicate on a scale of 1 to 10 the degree in which you love your mate in each of the areas. Then, when you have completed the evaluation scale, follow steps 1 through 4.

My dimension of agape love	*Degree of love*
1. Patience toward my mate	1 2 3 4 5 6 7 8 9 10
2. Kindness toward my mate	1 2 3 4 5 6 7 8 9 10
3. Lack of envy and jealousy	1 2 3 4 5 6 7 8 9 10
4. Lack of boasting (putting my mate down)	1 2 3 4 5 6 7 8 9 10
5. Lack of pride (competing with my mate)	1 2 3 4 5 6 7 8 9 10
6. Lack of rudeness	1 2 3 4 5 6 7 8 9 10
7. Not self-seeking (selfish behavior)	1 2 3 4 5 6 7 8 9 10
8. Not easily angered	1 2 3 4 5 6 7 8 9 10
9. Not keeping a record of wrongs	1 2 3 4 5 6 7 8 9 10
10. Not delighting in evil (insisting my mate participate in sinful actions)	1 2 3 4 5 6 7 8 9 10
11. Rejoicing in the truth (in doing God's will)	1 2 3 4 5 6 7 8 9 10
12. Protecting my mate	1 2 3 4 5 6 7 8 9 10
13. Trusting my mate	1 2 3 4 5 6 7 8 9 10
14. Seeing the best in my mate	1 2 3 4 5 6 7 8 9 10
15. Persevering in doing what is right	1 2 3 4 5 6 7 8 9 10

Step 1—Note the areas where you are *strongest*. Give yourself credit where credit is due.

Step 2—Note the items where you are *weakest*.

Step 3—Isolate the situations in your marital relationships where you demonstrate that weakness most.

Step 4—Set up one specific goal for each situation. For example, if you are quite frequently impatient, complete this sentence: This week I am going to demonstrate more patience toward my mate when . . .

Note: There may be legitimate reasons for your impatience. However, do not allow a two-way problem to keep you from working on your own negative reactions. If you begin to change, it often causes your mate to change too.

AS A COUPLE

Step 1—Each of you should complete the evaluation scales, Exercise 15, in *The Measure of a Marriage Workbook*.

Step 2—Each of you should also fill out the evaluation scale about your mate, Exercise 16.

Step 3—Compare your responses by filling out the comparative evaluation worksheets, Exercise 17. Put a plus (+) or a minus (−) in the box by each item to indicate if your mate rates you higher or lower than you do.

Step 4—Isolate areas of strength and weakness:

A.   Look for discrepancies between ''personal evaluation'' and your ''mate's evaluation of you.'' The items by which you placed a minus (−) will indicate the areas of discrepancies where you will need to concentrate. Plus (+) items indicate that you are harder on yourself than your mate is. Be encouraged!

Note: To be a significant discrepancy there should be two or more points difference. For example, if your mate circled number 5 regarding your "degree of patience" and you gave yourself a 6, consider this equal. However, if there's a two-point spread, consider this an area to look at carefully. Obviously, the greater the spread the greater the significance in difference and the more attention you should give that particular item.

B. In isolating areas of need, look for those items that are circled from 1 to 6; on a 10-point scale, consider 7 or above a very good score. However, if your scores mostly range at 7 or above, there is still room for improvement; but realize that if you rate this high with each other you are making great progress in learning to love.

Step 5—Each of you should record the answers to the questions listed in Exercise 18 in *The Measure of a Marriage Workbook*.

Step 6—Share what you've written with your mate either silently by letting him or her read what you have written or sharing it aloud.

Note: Decide together which approach you would rather use.

Step 7—Discuss together what you can do to help each other improve in your areas of weakness. Then write out specific goals in *The Measure of a Marriage Workbook*, Exercise 19.

AS A GROUP OF COUPLES

After reviewing the biblical material in the first part of this chapter, divide the total group into small groups. This time, however, include both men and women in each group, but have husbands in a different group than their wives. Have each group appoint a leader and a recorder.

Step 1—As a group answer the following questions which are based on the "dimension of *agape* love" scale on page 96.

1. What factors cause the most difficulty in the average marriage in keeping marital partners from demonstrating *patience* toward each other?

2. What factors cause the most difficulty in the average marriage in keeping marital partners from demonstrating *kindness* toward each other?

3. What causes *envy* in the average marriage?

4. What causes a marital partner to engage in *boasting* that has a negative effect in a marriage relationship?

5. What causes hurtful *pride?*

6. What causes *rude behavior* in a marital relationship?

7. What factors cause marital partners to be *selfish?*

8. What factors trigger hurtful *anger?*

9. Why do some marital partners keep *records of wrong?*

10. Why do some marital partners *delight in evil?*

11. What keeps a husband or wife from *rejoicing in the truth?*

12. Why do some marital partners *not protect* one another?

13. What destroys *trust* in a marriage?

14. What keeps marital partners from *seeing the best* in each other?

15. Why do some couples stop *persevering in doing what is right?*

Note: Allow about 15 minutes for this process. If you have several groups, have them divide up the questions. For example, half the group may start with question 1 and the rest of the group may start with question 15 and work backwards.

Step 2—Have the recorder share the group's observations and conclusions with the total group. If you have a number of groups, have each group recorder report on only one or two questions.

Couple Assignment
Ask each couple to work through the couple project outlined in the section for couples, and to complete Exercises 15, 16, 17, 18 and 19 in *The Measure of a Marriage Workbook*.

CHAPTER 11

Understanding Each Other

All human beings are unique—primarily because we are made in God's image. But beyond that, each of us is an individual. And as individuals we have *unique* needs, concerns, interests, talents and potentialities.

But there is yet another difference. We are uniquely male and female. Though both men and women reflect many similarities, we are indeed different in certain respects. And in order to meet one another's needs, we must understand one another, not only as individual human beings but as men and women.

Understanding Your Wife

The apostle Peter spoke directly to this issue in his first letter when he exhorted: ''You husbands likewise, live with your wives in an *understanding way*'' or literally, live with your wives "according to knowledge" (1 Pet. 3:7). From a practical point of view, Peter was saying that husbands are responsible before God to become *students* of their wives; to make a special effort to understand their particular uniqueness. This involves not only understanding them as individuals because they are human beings, but also as special people. Peter goes on to make this clear.

Your wife is "a woman." Live with your wife in an understanding way, continued Peter, "since she is a *woman.*"

Today, some people are attempting to eliminate unique distinctions between men and women. This is not only biblically unsound, but cannot be demonstrated pragmatically. True, there have been differentiations over the years that are absolutely absurd, unfair and unfounded. But certain distinctions are there nevertheless, even though men, particularly, have widened the gap far beyond reality. Though Adam first recognized Eve's humanness because of her *similarities* to him, he then discovered that she was uniquely *different* from him. She was a "woman" (Gen. 2:23).

Your wife is a "weaker vessel." Peter also stated something in this verse of Scripture that causes some women to actually see red. "Live with your wives in an understanding way," wrote Peter, "as with a *weaker vessel*" (1 Pet. 3:7).

One day I was lecturing on this subject in a well-known institution of higher learning. In the process a bright young woman put up her hand and asked, "Are you sure this is not some kind of translation error? Does the original language in the New Testament actually read 'a *weaker* vessel'?"

My answer had to be first no and then yes. No this is not a translation error. Yes it does mean a "weaker vessel" in the original New Testament text. In other words, this is what Peter actually said.

The problem is that some Bible interpreters have made Peter say far more than he meant. In fact, one very uninformed and prejudiced male once wrote, as he interpreted this phrase: "Women are weak in point of sex, the constitution of their body, mind and judgment, art, aptitude and wisdom in the conduct of affairs."

As a man, this statement embarrasses me. In fact, I hate to admit he is a fellow Bible interpreter. But unfortunately, some men actually believe this. But it is particularly true among men in non-Christian religions. For example, some Muslims actually believe that a woman does not have a soul. But how tragic when people who claim to believe the Bible teach such nonsense. The facts are that women often excel men in mental abilities, psychological and physical (women live longer) endurance, and in both scientific and artistic achievements.

What then does Peter actually mean? The answer is really quite simple. The apostle is referring to the degree of physical *strength* that women *normally* have when compared with men. Though there are exceptions, men by creation have more brute strength. This is easily observable in certain kinds of athletic activities today. Though women can often compete equally, and even exceed men in some sports—such as skiing and skating, you seldom see women able to hold their own against men in the more physically demanding sports such as basketball, football and hockey. Women, in this respect, are the "weaker vessels."

But some believe there is yet a deeper meaning in

Peter's statement. *Your wife is a sexual partner*. Some believe that the most basic and literal meaning of this verse has to do with "weaker vessel" in sexual intercourse. In other words, when Peter wrote, "*Live with* [dwell together with] your wives in an understanding way," he was first and foremost referring to the sexual relationship. Thus Peter would be saying, "Husbands, when you have sexual relations with your wives, do so with understanding and sensitivity remembering that she as a woman is not as strong as you are."

Personally, I would not restrict what Peter had in mind to this interpretation, though this kind of understanding is certainly inherent in what he says. Any Christian husband who is insensitive to his wife's physical capabilities in this most intimate area of life is indeed selfish and *not* understanding. And of course there's a great deal of variation among individual women in terms of actual physical strength and sexual responsiveness. This, too, must be considered if a Christian husband is to obey God and "live with his wife in an *understanding* way."

But just as important, if not more so, as understanding a woman's physical makeup is understanding her emotional needs. This certainly must be included in Peter's injunction. I say this because observations verify the importance of this again and again. I personally have seen many situations where a wife has been treated insensitively over a period of time, usually for several years. In turn she has attempted to tolerate the situation as best she could. Finally, however, her *feelings* of love die and either become numb or negative. In some instances she suddenly turns and walks away from the marriage, leaving her husband dumbfounded. When he asks her *why*, he discovers for the first time she has been feeling hurt and resentment for years because of his insensitivity to her feelings. "Why didn't you tell me?" he asks. "I tried to," she replies. "But you wouldn't listen. Now it's too late."

Unfortunately, when a woman really believes it's too late, it's very difficult to change her mind.

Obviously, most of these situations are two-way problems. The fault lies on both sides. But it does underscore *why* a husband *must* understand his wife.

Understanding Your Husband

Though Peter does not specifically tell wives "to live with their husbands in an understanding way," it is definitely implied in what he *does* say.

In chapter 3 verses 1-6 Peter specifically deals with a Christian wife's relationship to a non-Christian husband. This was a particular problem among those to whom Peter was writing. Evidently a number of women were becoming followers of Christ whereas their pagan husbands were not responding to the message of Christianity. Peter exhorted these women to be submissive to these men— that is, don't resist them or rebel. Furthermore, they were primarily to demonstrate the realities of Christianity with their life-style rather than with theological statements. They were definitely to be loyal to these men sexually, though some certainly were tempted to become involved with Christian men who would be more understanding and sensitive. And, rather than emphasizing *external* adornment, they were to demonstrate true *inner* qualities—"a gentle and quiet spirit."

Peter's specific instructions to these women involves behavior on their part that reflects keen insight into the unique male personality. Ironically, men have often been classified as being superior to women. In this passage Peter implies that in at least one area of life men seem to be inferior, particularly in terms of ego strength.

The male ego is a very sensitive dimension in every man. Though it often reflects strength, it is frequently a cover-up for weakness and feelings of insecurity. A woman who either attacks a male ego or ignores it is only aggravating the problem. She certainly is not living with her husband in an "understanding way."

Peter, it seems, was by implication treating this aspect of the male personality. He exhorted these women to be sensitive to this unique problem. Just as a husband is to be sensitive to a woman's lack of *physical* strength, so a woman is to be sensitive to a man's lack of *ego* strength.

This observation has been verified again and again in my own counseling experiences with couples who are having difficulty in their relationship. A woman who attacks or ignores a man's ego needs can in some instances actually incapacitate him. For example, he may not be able to perform sexually; or if he can perform, he is not able to do so sensitively and compassionately. Furthermore, he may become withdrawn and uncommunicative; or he may become angry or resentful, which interferes with his ability to be emotionally sensitive and understanding.

In these situations a man is also extremely vulnerable. He is easily tempted into an extramarital affair by a woman who *understands* his ego needs. Ironically, most successful prostitutes are masters at understanding men in this area of their lives. And this also explains why some men—even Christian men—will give up everything—a good Christian woman, children, a home, position and finances—to live with another woman. At that moment in his life, more important to him than anything else in the whole world, even his Christianity, is that his ego needs be met. This is tragic but true! I've seen it happen to some of my acquaintances.

A vital relationship with Jesus Christ can of course change a man. But conversion to Christianity and a desire to live according to God's will does not automatically eliminate the problem every man has with his nature which he inherited from Adam. This was why Peter turned next (3:7) to *Christian* husbands and exhorted them to live with their wives in an ''understanding way'' and to grant them ''honor as a fellow-heir of the grace of life.''

But as with every relationship in life, this is a two-way street. Every man needs a woman who understands more than anything his ego needs. And every woman needs a man who understands her uniqueness as a woman. And through mutual understanding they can grow together, meeting each other's needs, whatever those needs might be.

Peter concluded his instructions to people in general and to husbands and wives in particular: ''To sum up, let all be harmonious, sympathetic, brotherly, kind-hearted, and humble in spirit; not returning evil for evil, or insult for insult, but giving a blessing instead; for you were called for the very purpose that you might inherit a blessing'' (1 Pet. 3:8,9).

CHAPTER 12

An Exercise in Developing Feeling Love

We have already considered three dimensions of love which are discussed and illustrated in the Bible (see fig. 1, p. 94). Generally speaking, *agape* love involves doing what is right and best for someone even if it involves negative feelings. *Phileo* love often refers to that dimension of love that involves responding to someone's needs affectionately and with positive emotions. *Erao* love involves sexual response.

Though there are many instances when we must demonstrate love at the action level even when we don't feel like it (that is, if a marriage is to work), it is not God's will that our lives together as husbands and wives be characterized primarily by negative feelings. Rather, we are to *enjoy* each other; not merely endure a painful relationship.

Probably 99 percent of all men and women in our culture enter marriage with very positive feelings. Unfortunately, these feelings are often more physically oriented rather than reflecting a love that is comprehensive and based on mature understanding and feelings. Fortunately, many of these couples soon learn to love each other at a deeper level. On the other hand, what began as a strong physical attraction, in some instances, subsides rather quickly or very quickly turns to feelings of resentment and anger.

How can a marriage, no matter at what level it began in terms of love, grow and mature at the *feeling* level? The answer to this question is to live together in an understanding way. It is only as we come to know each other emotionally that we can minister to each other emotionally. This involves learning to communicate at the *feeling* level. The following exercise is designed to help you accomplish that goal.

AS AN INDIVIDUAL

If your marital partner is uninterested in communication at this level, you have before you a difficult challenge. But don't give up until you give it your best shot. Maybe your mate does not understand your feelings because you don't understand his or hers.

Step 1—Determine what areas create the most difficulty in your marital communication. Respond to the following questions as honestly as possible:

1. Write down several areas where you communicate well with your mate. That is, you can discuss matters together and reach conclusions objectively, clearly and with understanding.

2. Write down several areas where you have difficulty communicating with your mate. That is, you feel these areas usually create misunderstanding and emotional difficulties.

3. Write down areas where you feel you communicate with your mate very superficially or not at all.

Step 2—Analyze your communication style. How do you come across to your mate? Are you a *positive* or a *negative* communicator? The following exercise will help you with this personal evaluation. Check the box in front of each statement to indicate which approach more frequently characterizes your communication style.

When You State Your Opinions or Desires . . .[1]

Do you say:	or	*Do you say:*
☐ Pick up your ...		☐ Would you please be kind enough to ...?
☐ Why don't you...?		☐ Have you thought about trying ...?
☐ Let's go ...		☐ How would you feel about going ...?
☐ There must be a better way to do that.		☐ Perhaps you would do better if you ...
☐ You sure know how to hurt me.		☐ I'm glad you let me know exactly how you feel.
☐ Don't pry so much.		☐ I'm glad you feel free to ask that kind of question even though it is painful for me.
☐ Thanks for doing ...		☐ You certainly did a good job on that.

Do you say: or	*Do you say:*
☐ I'm glad you finally got that job done.	☐ I admire the way you use your time to complete jobs like …
☐ I'm glad you finally…	☐ It was very thoughtful of you to …
☐ I'm glad we have finally gone out to dinner.	☐ I enjoyed eating out so much. Thanks for taking me there.
☐ Thanks for the meal.	☐ You're a wonderful cook. Dinner was delicious.

Note: Remember, you are automatically a negative communicator if you don't say anything when you could express appreciation in a positive manner.

In view of this little exercise, how would you classify your communication style? Is it more positive than negative? Is it more negative than positive? *Your goal should be to become as sincerely positive as possible.* When this happens you will be amazed at the changes that will take place in your mate.

Note: Do not be manipulative. This is why I said to be *sincerely* positive. And remember! You can be sincere even though you may have to force yourself emotionally to be positive. The more you practice, the easier and more natural it will become. And once you are positively reinforced by your mate because you have been positive, the process will become even more natural and easy.

AS A COUPLE
An Initial Exercise:

Step 1—It is important that you as a couple learn how to share and exchange feelings. To achieve this goal, spend 15 minutes separately making observations in Exercise 20 of *The Measure of a Marriage Workbook*.

Step 2—Now that you have recorded your responses to these questions on your worksheets, share your answers with each other by reading what your mate has written. Then discuss your answers beginning with question 1. Then move to question 2, and finally question 3. Note differences in opinion as well as agreement. Try to discover why the differences exist.

Step 3—Analyze your communication style with your mate by using Exercise 21 in *The Measure of a Marriage Workbook*.

Step 4—Now that each of you has completed the exercise for evaluating your own communication style with your mate, evaluate your mate's communication style by completing Exercise 22 in your workbook.

Step 5—Compare *your* evaluation of your own communication style with your *mate's* evaluation of your communication style. Do so by completing the comparative worksheets, Exercise 23 in your workbook.

Step 6—Use the comparative worksheets you have just completed to analyze how you view your own communication style compared with how your mate views your communication style. Isolate areas of agreement and disagreement. Discuss why this disagreement exists and *how* you can become more sensitive and understanding in your communication with each other.

Step 7—Now that you have completed the preceding steps, turn to Exercise 24 in *The Measure of a Marriage Workbook*. There are several duplicate exercises on which you and your spouse can share and express your feelings. Follow through on this exercise for at least *seven* days. You may write in your answers and let your mate read your responses out loud if you have difficulty verbalizing them. If necessary, consult the list of positive and negative emotions that follow.

Positive Feelings	*Negative Feelings*
Pleased	Anxious
Understanding	Fear
Hopeful	Lonely
Tenderness	Uncertainty
Proud	Insecure
Closeness	Confusion
Excited	Sad
Happiness	Rejection
Contented	Angry
Confident	Bored
Acceptance	Helplessness
Grateful	Scared
Affectionate	Frustrated
Sexual arousal	Frigidity
Eager	Foolish
Elated	Confused
Calm	Apathetic

Note: It may be necessary in your marriage to continue this process indefinitely. In fact, it is a good exercise to make good marriages even better.

AS A GROUP OF COUPLES

After reviewing the biblical material at the beginning of this chapter, have your group or groups concentrate on how to become positive communicators. Again, divide your groups to include both men and women, and have each group appoint a group leader and a group recorder.

Step 1—Have each group utilize the evaluation form on pages 76,78 in the Workbook, which demonstrates positive and negative communication styles. Read through this material with the total group. Then have each small group add additional illustrations which contrast negative and positive communication.

Step 2—Have each group recorder share several of the group's illustrations.

Step 3—If there is time following the group reports, allow for any questions or comments regarding the process the group has gone through.

Couple Assignment

Ask each couple to work through the couple project outlined in the section for couples, using Exercises 20,21,22,23 and 24 in *The Measure of a Marriage Workbook*.

Suggested Listening Assignment: Secure a set of Dr. Ed Wheat's two cassette tapes entitled *Love Life* (available in your local Christian bookstore). Dr. Wheat makes excellent suggestions regarding how to restore lost feelings in your marriage.

Note

1. Adapted from Mort Katz, *Marriage Survival Kit* (New York: Farnsworth Publishing Co., 1974), p. 39.

CHAPTER 13

Meeting Each Other's Sexual Needs

No concept is clearer in the Bible than the fact that men are designed by God to meet a woman's sexual needs, and vice versa. For many people this sets up a tension. Historically, human beings have not done too well at resolving it, primarily because they are unaware of God's total perspective on marriage as revealed in the Bible. And, if they *are aware* of His divine guidelines, they refuse to follow them. Unfortunately for us we cannot ignore God's laws without suffering the consequences. Though the initial results of disobedience may be emotionally rewarding, the ultimate results, even in this life, are always disappointing and often devastating.

To this point in our study we've been looking at God's *total* perspective on marriage. This is vital because it is impossible to comprehend sexual function and to be a satisfying as well as satisfied sexual partner unless we have this enlarged perspective. All the sex manuals in the world will not solve sex problems and improve sexual relations on a long-term basis—

- unless the husband and wife are in the process of becoming one emotionally and spiritually;
- unless they have "left father and mother" emotionally and spiritually;
- unless they are learning to love as Christ loved;
- unless they are experiencing mutual submission;
- unless they are learning to love at both the action and feeling levels;
- unless they are learning to understand each other not only as male and female but as unique individuals.

It is only as a husband and wife practice these principles in marriage that they can enjoy sexual expression as God intended. These divine guidelines provide the foundation that causes sexual enjoyment in marriage to endure and improve. Furthermore, they also enable a husband and wife to keep subtle selfish desires from destroying what God intended to be a mutually satisfying experience.

Before discussing specific ways we can become better sexual partners, let's look at what God says first about moral purity and then about meeting each other's sexual needs.

Moral Commitment

Once two people marry, God's laws protect that marriage. It has been that way from the beginning of creation. God made these laws absolutely clear when He thundered His commandments from Mount Sinai (see Exod. 20:14, 17).

"You shall not commit adultery." The world at large

has never accepted this law. It is often a common practice for a married man to engage in sexual relations on a regular basis with women other than his wife.

One evening my wife and I were having dinner in the home of a young man (an American) and his wife who had been born and reared in another culture. The conversation turned to the life-style in her country, particularly relative to sexual mores. When I quizzed the young woman about some specific behaviors among married men and how it would affect their marriages, she responded, "Oh, wives in our culture are very tolerant of their husbands."

In essence she was expressing a fact that has been prevalent for centuries in many parts of the world that have not been significantly influenced by Hebrew/ Christian values. In reality, she was saying that these women had very little choice, especially if they wanted to survive economically and socially. It is a part of the cultural system for a man to have more than one woman in his life and wives can do little but accept it as a reality.

In fact, in some parts of the first-century culture, wives could actually have been sentenced to death by their husbands for overtly rebelling against their free-wheeling and permissive life-styles. When Paul and others began preaching the gospel of Christ in the first-century pagan culture, these New Testament Christian leaders encountered some of these conditions. But along with the message of salvation, they taught a new ethic—actually an old ethic—relative to marriage. According to the will of God, a Christian husband and wife were to be loyal to each other sexually. There were to be no intimate relationships outside of their marriage.

"Be . . . the husband of one wife." When Paul wrote to Timothy who was in Ephesus and to Titus who was in

Crete, he stated the qualifications for spiritual leaders in the church. In both passages of Scripture, being the "husband of one wife" stands out at the top of the list (1 Tim. 3:2; Titus 1:6).

What did Paul mean? Actually, the phrase "husband of one wife" can also be translated "man of one woman." In fact, this phrase may express Paul's original meaning more adequately. You see it was very common for a man living in the New Testament culture to have not only a wife but other girls he visited regularly for sexual gratification. There was frequently the prostitute at the local temple. Also, he may have had access to a slave girl who was considered a part of the household. In most instances, his wife was well-aware of his extramarital involvements. The other girls were for fun and games. Her place was to care for the house and to bear children and rear them. And there was actually very little she could do about the situation. She had few alternatives in her culture. It was a fact of life.

But the message and impact of Christianity brought change. In fact, from the beginning of time God planned for a man to have only one woman in his life and He planned for a woman to have only one man in her life. Though He allowed Old Testament personalities to violate this divine plan it was not within His perfect will. And whenever the plan *was* violated, it caused jealousy, fostered disunity, brought heartache and created other difficulties. This is abundantly illustrated in the life of such Old Testament characters as Abraham, Jacob, David and Solomon.

"Every one who looks on a woman to lust for her" commits adultery. The message of Christianity not only reinforced God's initial plan but established an even

higher standard of morality. When confronting the Pharisees regarding the relationship between a husband and wife, Jesus told them that to actually look on a woman and to lust after her was the same—in God's eyes—as already committing adultery in the heart. In other words, it was not necessarily the *act* of sexual intercourse that was adultery, but also the very *plan* to engage in this activity (see Matt. 5:27,28).

Don't misunderstand. Jesus was not saying that every time a man (or a woman) is tempted sexually it is sin. Unfortunately, Jimmy Carter, when he was candidating for the presidency of the United States, seems to have misunderstood the difference between "lust" as Jesus used the word and "temptation." You'll remember the much publicized comment that he made regarding the fact that he probably commits adultery in his heart every day, referring back to Jesus' statement in Matthew's Gospel. Understandably, *Playboy* and other pornographic magazines had a heyday over the statement. What Mr. Carter should have said and hopefully what he meant, to be biblically accurate, was that he is probably *tempted* every day. And to be tempted per se is not committing adultery of the heart. Adultery as Jesus defined it is when a man or woman actually look *and* plan to engage in a sexual act with someone other than his or her marital partner. The moment a person moves in that direction, the intent to engage in a sexual act becomes adultery in God's eyes.

Every Christian man and woman must be on guard against this kind of behavior. Looking—particularly pro-longed looking and thinking—can easily lead to lust as Jesus defined it. Temptation can quickly become sin. We're all tempted if we're human at all. This is particularly true for men who are usually more visually oriented than women. And living in a culture that uses every means possible to tap these natural capacities creates many situations every day that are tempting. However, we need not sin against God or our marital partners. We need not lust. With God's help we can refocus our thoughts. And part of this divine plan in marriage is that sexual needs are to be met regularly within the bonds of marriage.

Engaging in Regular Sexual Relations

The Bible clearly and forthrightly teaches that regular sexual relationships are designed by God to be a natural and normal part of marriage. The apostle Paul probably spoke more specifically in this regard than any other biblical author. When writing to the Corinthians he stated: "Let the husband fulfill his duty to his wife, and likewise also the wife to her husband. The wife does not have authority over her own body, but the husband does; and likewise also the husband does not have authority over his own body, but the wife does. Stop depriving one another, except by agreement for a time that you may devote yourselves to prayer, and come together again lest Satan tempt you because of your lack of self-control" (1 Cor. 7:3-5).

To understand the reasons why Paul in this instance was so outspoken about sex and marriage, we must understand some historical and cultural factors. The city of Corinth was noted even in the pagan Roman world for its low morals. During Paul's day it was a large and growing city with a population well over 100,000 people. However, its population was mobile, consisting of traveling businessmen, sailors, and government officials. Illicit sexual behavior was rampant.

To add to Corinth's moral degradation, religious prostitution was a part of its cultic practice. History records that in New Testament times at least 1,000 priestesses were employed in religious prostitution and operated out of the temple of Aphrodite. Readily accessible and always available, they provided any kind of sexual experience any man (or woman) wanted—day or night.

It was in this environment that Paul preached the gospel of Jesus Christ on his second missionary journey. Rejected by many of his fellow Jews, he turned to the pagan Gentiles in that city. Luke records that "many of the Corinthians when they heard were believing and being baptized" (Acts 18:8). Consequently, those who made up the church at Corinth were mostly pagan people, many of whom were converted to Christ out of a life of prostitution, adulterous relationships, homosexuality, and a variety of criminal acts. In fact, Paul makes this very clear in his first letter to the Corinthian Christians when he said: "Do not be deceived: Neither the sexually immoral nor idolaters nor adulterers nor male prostitutes nor homosexual offenders nor thieves nor the greedy nor drunkards nor slanderers nor swindlers will inherit the kingdom of God. *And that is what some of you were*" (1 Cor. 6:9-11, *NIV*).

Ascetic Practices

There was yet another problem in Corinth. There were some religious philosophers who were teaching ascetic practices which included the doctrine that it is better not to marry; consequently abstaining from *all* sexual activity. This philosophy also influenced these new Christians in Corinth. Some of these believers evidently erroneously syncretized Paul's teaching on morality with this pagan practice. And since most of these Christians were no doubt already married, they attempted to practice sexual abstinence within the marriage state, thinking it would make them more acceptable to God. Perhaps their previous immoral life-style caused them to overreact to Paul's teaching on morality. Furthermore, some of these pagan philosophers probably began to proselytize these new Christians.

Paul faced this problem by acknowledging the unmarried state as good and proper *if* a person felt this was his gift from God (see 1 Cor. 7:7-9). And this would be especially true if a person felt he could maintain a life of moral purity as a single person living in the midst of a very immoral environment (see 1 Cor. 7:1,2). But then Paul made it very clear that God designed marriage as a legitimate context in which men and women could and should express sexual feelings openly, freely and without a sense of guilt. Furthermore, Paul pointed out to the Corinthians that since their questions involved men and women who were already married, they were in no way to withhold sex from their marital partners. If they did, Paul warned, they would be setting the stage for Satan to tempt one or the other into an illicit sexual affair.

We see then that the Bible is very practical in the area of sex. In essence, God is saying that people *do* have sexual needs. Furthermore, marriage is the place for these needs to be met. And each marital partner is responsible to make sure those needs *are* met. If they should decide to abstain sexually for a time, it should be agreed upon by both, but only on a temporary basis and for spiritual reasons. Note however that Paul is not correlating the *absence* of sex as being a means per se to more holiness. Rather, abstaining temporarily would simply allow more concentrated time for prayer.

The Universal Principle

Inherent in Paul's instructions to the Corinthians, who were facing some particular problems in their own culture, is a universal principle that applies to every marriage since the time of Adam and Eve. When a man and woman choose to be joined together in holy matrimony, they take upon themselves a special responsibility to meet each other's sexual needs. Paraphrasing Paul, since their bodies now belong to each other, they are not to "withhold" sex from each other.

We must quickly add, however, that it is important to interpret this injunction in the light of other God-given directives and principles in Scripture which relate to marriage and which have been discussed in previous chapters. Paul's exhortation to the Corinthians, if taken out of the total context of Scripture, can be used selfishly and insensitively. And used in this way it can literally destroy a marital partner emotionally, and eventually the marriage itself.

The Circle of Biblical Love

The principles outlined in our previous chapters can be summarized by once again looking at a biblical definition of love (see fig. 1, p. 94). Most references to love in the New Testament do not refer to sexual expression per se. Rather, most refer to *agapao* love—doing what is *right* and *best* for someone, even if it involves negative feelings. Closely aligned with *agapao* love is *phileo* love—responding to someone's needs affectionately and with positive emotions, but always within the guidelines of *agapao* love. For the most part, it is God's will that *agapao* and *phileo* love overlap. But the Bible clearly assumes that there are times when we must do things for someone because it is right, not because we necessarily desire to do so.

This poses a problem when it comes to *erao* love, which involves physical and emotional involvement with another person sexually. Men particularly and generally cannot function sexually without erotic feelings. Unfortunately, however, a man can experience these erotic feelings purely at a selfish level and with any woman who is sexually available. Putting it simply, it is easy for a man to engage in erotic "love" outside the circle of biblical love (see fig. 1, p. 94). The history of female prostitution affirms this point.

In some respects, women have the same capability, but not to the same extent as men. This is why most biblical injunctions regarding moral purity are directed at men (see Exod. 20:17; Matt. 5:28; 1 Tim. 3:2; Titus 1:6). It is a fact of life, generally speaking, that men *are* more visually and erotically oriented when it comes to sex. They are more easily aroused, more physically oriented and more vulnerable to temptation. Every modern-day advertising agency is well-aware of this reality.

Women, on the other hand, are more emotionally oriented. Though they are very capable of being intensely erotic, they usually respond sexually to a man who provides them with security, who understands their deep feelings, who is sensitive, tender and compassionate. Their extramarital affairs are normally precipitated because they are angry, lonesome, insecure or generally unhappy and unfulfilled.

Note: Men are also vulnerable when these emotional states occur. However, a man may also choose to engage in extramarital sex simply because he has a physical need. This is not to say that some women may not do the same thing. But it is usually the exception, not the rule.

What does all of this mean in a marriage where both the husband and wife are committed to *Christian* values? The following chapter is designed to answer this question.

CHAPTER 14

An Exercise in Developing Sexual Love

Getting to know each other sexually in a marital relationship is one of the great adventures God has designed for husbands and wives. Though creativity in this area of a couple's life must be sensitively developed within the context of both *agapao* (action) and *phileo* (feeling) love, it nevertheless provides in itself a lifelong challenge. Like any activity in life, sexual relationships can become routine and meaningless for any couple. This chapter is designed to help you keep this area of your life interesting, challenging and mutually satisfying.

AS AN INDIVIDUAL

How well do you understand your mate as a sexual being? The following questions and explanations will help you answer this question. Notice that there is a section for wives as well as a section for husbands. Since men and women differ in their sexual makeup, it is important to understand these differences.

As a Wife
How well do I understand my husband's sexual nature?

Most men are quite consistent in their sexual makeup. There are exceptions, of course, but generally when you understand one man, you understand them all. Following are some key insights to help you understand the average husband:

- Sexually, he is visually oriented.

- He can be sexually aroused almost instantaneously.

- His sexual drive is closely related to the ebb and flow of glandular fluids.
    Note: A sexually active man cannot suddenly turn off his sexual desire. It has now become a spontaneous physiological process. Once he has become used to regular sexual emissions, prostate fluid is produced accordingly.

- A man's ego is closely aligned with what his wife thinks about him sexually. For example, a man whose wife demonstrates negative attitudes toward his genitals feels intensely rejected as a total person.

How aware am I of my husband's sexual temptations?

- Most women who dress provocatively arouse a man sexually. Because the average woman in the average office in today's work-a-day world dresses provocatively, the average husband—even the Christian husband—is, to a certain extent, sexually stimulated nearly every day—and by more than one woman.

• Most advertising today, whether it is in the newspapers, magazines, TV or radio, is designed to arouse a man sexually. Since we live in a media-oriented world, it is almost impossible for the average man to avoid some kind of erotic stimulation on a regular basis.

• The degree of arousal in the average man varies, depending on several factors. But one of the most significant factors relates to the extent of his sexual fulfillment with his wife and particularly the regularity of sexual release.

Note: A man who gives himself over to lustful behavior as a way of life is never satisfied sexually. However, even a man who attempts to abide by God's standards faces regular sexual temptations, and experiences continual sexual needs.

How understanding am I of my husband's temptations?

Some women resent their husband's sexual nature. Remember that the average *Christian* husband feels guilty already regarding his weaknesses in this area of his life. To feel resentment and lack of understanding from his wife only adds to his own feelings of self-condemnation and guilt. In fact, this kind of attitude often accentuates his vulnerability to other women who *do* understand his nature, accept it and use it to their advantage.

How available am I to my husband sexually?

• Because you do not feel sexual desire does not mean your husband does not.

• Demonstrating "unavailability" does not diminish your husband's sexual drive; in fact, it may increase it.

• When your husband reads your "unavailable" signals and withdraws, it does not mean he has forgotten what he feels.

• A wise wife learns how to meet her husband's sexual needs even when it is inconvenient for her personally (during pregnancy, menstrual periods, etc.).

• When it is necessary to abstain totally, a wise wife learns how to say no without making her husband feel rejected.

What can I do to make myself more physically attractive?
   Remember: Most women do not have to undergo physical surgery to become more attractive. Remarkable changes can result from some do-it-yourself projects:

• Avoiding excessive weight

• Bathing regularly—especially before lovemaking

• Using cosmetics effectively

• Dressing appropriately for the bedroom.

What can I do to become a more creative lover?
   Note: Most people (men included) do not become creative lovers naturally. It takes thought and practice. Following are the great inhibitors in this process:

• Negative attitudes toward sex

• Inappropriate information

• Lack of information

• Thinking only of oneself.

Remember: God has designed marriage for one man and one woman. Beyond that He does not lock us into sexual forms. The very nature of both men's and women's physical and emotional makeup makes sex one of the areas of life for the greatest opportunity for creative exploration.

What can I do to set the stage for a pleasant environment for lovemaking?

The physical environment is important to a man. An unattractive bedroom or even poor housekeeping habits generally affect a man's feelings about sex. However, also remember that the emotional environment is just as important (if not more so) than the physical environment. Nothing is more disappointing to a man than negative attitudes in a beautiful bedroom.

Do I really know and understand what my husband likes and dislikes about our lovemaking? Do I make it easy for him to talk about it?

As a Husband
How well do I understand my wife's sexual nature?

It's important to realize that individual women vary far more in their sexual makeup than the average man. On the one hand, a small percentage of women have a high degree of natural sexual desire. On the other hand, a small percentage of women have a low degree of natural sexual desire. However, the majority of women fall somewhere in the middle. The facts are that many women can live comfortably (from a purely physiological point of view) without engaging in intimate sexual relationships. In this sense they differ noticeably from men.

Don't misunderstand. This does not mean women cannot and do not enjoy sex—even those with a low sex drive. It does mean, however, that their nature is different. If a man does not understand this, he can be very threatened. Furthermore, his expectation levels regarding his wife and himself become very unrealistic.

Following are several things to remember about the *average* woman.

• Whereas men are visually oriented, women are more oriented to what they sense and feel.

• Whereas the man is normally quickly aroused (even at a distance), a woman is normally aroused gradually and in a context of understanding, sensitivity and appropriate physical touch and stimulation.

• Whereas a man's sexual drive is correlated with the ebb and flow of his own body fluids (internal stimulation), a woman's sexual drive is correlated more significantly with external stimuli; namely, a warm accepting and understanding relationship with her husband.

Note: Many women experience degrees of difference in their sexual response depending on their menstrual cycle. However, the phenomenon is far different than male secretionary processes and how they affect sexual desire and arousal.

• Whereas a man's ego is closely aligned with his sexual performance, a woman's sexual performance relates more to her sense of pride and psychological need to be an adequate sexual partner.

What can I do to help my wife be more responsive sexually?

Since a woman's sexual response is usually triggered differently than a man's, careful attention should be given to the following:

• Don't expect your wife to be ready to engage in sex just because you are.

• Don't be threatened by her initial lack of desire.

• Think of ways to make sexual response more natural and easier for your wife. Following are some suggestions:

1. Remember that sexual feelings in a woman can begin to be aroused a long time before sexual intercourse—actually many hours before. This is often caused by sharing loving and tender feelings. This causes a woman to feel understood, secure and accepted.

2. Demonstrate your love to your wife unconditionally and consistently. In other words, don't compartmentalize sexual activity. Make it a part of numerous expressions of love.

Note: Some men only say "I love you" and show affection and do nice things for their wives only when they are interested in sex. This is a turn-off for many women. They feel bribed and used.

3. Plan lovemaking at a time when your wife is physically and emotionally fresh.

Note: A long day with the kids in a closed environment is not very conducive to stimulating a sexual response. Be understanding about these circumstances. Plan ways to circumvent these problems.

• Learn to know your wife's physical and psychological makeup as an individual woman. What pleases her? What kind of physical stimulation aids her in being sexually satisfied?

Caution: What may please your wife on one occasion may not on another. Furthermore, what pleases other women may not necessarily please your wife. Remember too that a woman is not as consistent in her response to certain stimuli as men. Don't let this confuse you or threaten you. Take it as a challenge and learn to know the many moods of your wife and her uniqueness as a woman.

Do I know and understand what my wife is feeling?

This is basic to feminine sexual response. Feelings of resentment, anger, insecurity, fear, etc., are all great inhibitors in causing a woman *not* to respond sexually.

Listen to your wife's feelings. Encourage her to share how she feels. Accept those feelings. Try not to take personally her negative feelings toward you as a husband. These are normal and natural. Though it is sometimes painful, remember that she will love you for it.

How can I be more tender toward my wife?

Mort Katz in his *Marriage Survival Kit*[1] suggests the following will help you develop this quality in your marital relationship:

- Tenderness is asking your wife what she is feeling.

- Tenderness is asking your wife what she means.

- Tenderness is telling your wife that you understand how she feels.

- Tenderness is telling your wife you are glad for her happiness when she is happy.

- Tenderness is telling your wife you are sorry for her pain when she's hurting inside.

- Tenderness is hugging your wife apart from sexual relationships.

- Tenderness is holding your wife gently when she's hurting.

- Tenderness is sharing your happy feelings with your wife.

- Tenderness is letting your wife know what you enjoy and appreciate about her.

- Tenderness is hanging up your clothes neatly.

- Tenderness is taking out the garbage.

- Tenderness is paying the bills.

- Tenderness is helping your wife with her household responsibilities when she asks for help.

- Tenderness is tuning into your wife's true feelings.

How can I become more physically attractive to my wife?

It is true that men are far more easily aroused sexually through what they see, but women find it more difficult as well to be aroused by a physically unattractive husband. The same basic suggestions given to wives also apply to you in making yourself physically more attractive.

- Get rid of excessive weight.

- Bathe regularly.

- Smell good.

And remember: Don't let it threaten you if your wife is not as sexually aroused by your physical manner as much as you are aroused by her feminine mystique.

AS A COUPLE

Warning! As you begin this process as a couple, your greatest challenge is being sensitive in the communication that lies before you. You're venturing into the most vulnerable area of your inner being. Be honest and yet kind and gentle. Remember too that if you do not measure up in these areas as you think you do or as much as you want to, it will be a great opportunity for developing both understanding and skill as a sexual partner. Though you may be initially threatened, great dividends can eventually come.

Note: If you reach an impasse in communication, you may need to seek help from an objective third party who is skilled in marital counseling.

Step 1—Complete the "Evaluation Scale for Wives" and the "Evaluation Scale for Husbands," Exercise 25 in *The Measure of a Marriage Workbook*.

Step 2—Complete the evaluation scales in Exercise 26 in *The Measure of a Marriage Workbook*.

Step 3—Fill in the comparative forms, Exercise 27 in *The Measure of a Marriage Workbook*.

Step 4—Together isolate areas of agreement and disagreement on the comparative forms. Note that a one-point variance on a five-point scale may be significant.

Step 5—In addition to areas of disagreement, also note obvious areas of low understanding. Use these areas to go back and read the information that corresponds with these areas on pages 129-137 in this book, *The Measure of a Marriage*.

Together read through both sets of questions and explanations. Flip a coin to see who goes first.

As a Wife (if you're first): Read out loud to your husband the section designed for you and entitled "As a Wife." Following each question and the explanations, stop and ask your husband if he agrees with the author's observations and suggestions.

As a Husband: Read out loud to your wife the section entitled "As a Husband." Following each question and the explanations, stop and ask your wife if she agrees with the author's observations and suggestions.

Step 6 : Conclude this process together by participating in a positive interaction exercise suggested by David and Vera Mace in their excellent book entitled, *How to Have a Happy Marriage*.[2]

Sit facing each other and hold hands if you are comfortable in doing so. Tell each other some of the things about each other that you really appreciate.

Instead of a back and forth dialogue, decide who will go first, then take only one turn each. Look into each other's eyes while you talk, and address each other directly by name. Do the exercise in a reflective, unhurried way, with pauses wherever you like. During your turn, think of a number of qualities in your partner and share them slowly one by one, beginning each with "I love you because . . ."; or "I like you when . . ."; "Another thing I especially like about you is . . ."; or similar words that come naturally to you.

Take plenty of time with this exercise, and talk about it afterwards—how you felt, how you reacted to what was said to you. Furthermore, once you have gone through this experience, do it again from time to time—not often enough to make it routine, but as something to be reserved for special occasions.

AS A GROUP OF COUPLES

After reviewing the biblical material in chapter 13, divide the group into smaller groups. This time go back to the previous organizational structure. Have women with women in groups and men with men. Have each group appoint leaders and recorders.

Step 1—Before the individual groups go to work, read out loud the questions and observations in the first section of this exercise on pages 130-137.

Step 2—After you read the material out loud, instruct the groups to do the following:

Husbands' Groups: Respond to the section entitled "As a Wife," beginning on page 130. Ask for any comments they would like to make regarding the author's material. What additional questions would they ask and what additional observations would they make?

Wives' Groups: Respond to the section entitled "As a Husband," beginning on page 133. Ask for any comments they would like to make regarding the author's observations. What additional questions and explanations would they like to make?

Step 3—Have each group recorder share with the total group, avoiding repetition.

Couple Assignment

Following the group process, ask each couple to go home and personalize this group project in their own marriage by working through the projects designed for couples in this text and in *The Measure of a Marriage Workbook,* Exercises 25, 26 and 27.

For Further Reading: Read *Intended for Pleasure* by Dr. Ed Wheat and his wife Gaye Wheat (published by Fleming H. Revell). Dr. Wheat is a family physician and in this book he and his wife write very specifically regarding techniques that can improve your sexual relationship.

Dr. Wheat has also prepared two cassette tapes entitled *Sex Techniques* and *Sex Problems* (available from your local bookstore). Dr. Wheat will provide you with three hours of intimate personal sex counsel to enrich your marital life.

Just a Beginning

Though we've reached the end of this *book,* it is really just a beginning. Growing in a marriage relationship must be continuous and ongoing. In fact, it would be well for you to actually start over again and work through all the projects once more. You'll discover that your life together can deepen indefinitely.

Better yet, share the process with someone else. As a couple start a marriage enrichment class for other couples. Guide them through the projects designed for a group of couples, which will in turn launch them into the couples' projects—which you'll want to go through again yourself.

Notes

1. Adapted from Mort Katz, *Marriage Survival Kit* (New York: Farnsworth Publishing Co., 1974), p. 61.
2. David and Vera Mace, *How to Have a Happy Marriage* (Nashville: Abingdon Press, 1977), p. 126.